THE EMPOWERED EMPLOYEE

THE EMPOWERED EMPLOYEE

PRACTICAL WAYS TO GAIN AN EDGE AT THE WORKPLACE

SERINA SIDHU

Notion Press

Old No. 38, New No. 6
McNichols Road, Chetpet
Chennai - 600 031

First Published by Notion Press 2016
Copyright © Serina Sidhu 2016
All Rights Reserved.

ISBN 978-1-946129-49-9

This book has been published with all efforts taken to make the material error-free after the consent of the author. However, the author and the publisher do not assume and hereby disclaim any liability to any party for any loss, damage, or disruption caused by errors or omissions, whether such errors or omissions result from negligence, accident, or any other cause.

No part of this book may be used, reproduced in any manner whatsoever without written permission from the author, except in the case of brief quotations embodied in critical articles and reviews.

Dedication

I dedicate this book, to the fond memory of my parents. Wing Commander Devinder Sidhu, a highly acclaimed pilot in the Indian Air Force. Recognized for his leadership, and public speaking skills, his strong sense of self-belief and passion for the unknown have been a tremendous source of motivation in my first book-writing initiative, and my mother Mrs. Teresa Sidhu, who encouraged and supported me every step of the way to accomplish all my desired goals and objectives.

Contents

Special Thanks to…   ix
Testimonial   xi
Author's Preview   xiii
About the Author   xv
Acknowledgement   xvii

1. Find the Perfect Job   1
2. Pre-Interview Guidelines   7
3. Ace Your Interview   12
4. Develop Strong Leadership Skills   27
5. Write an Effective résumé a Résumé Speaks   33
6. Create a Professional Cover Letter   46
7. Build a Positive Mental Attitude   53
8. Emotional Intelligence (EQ)   56
9. Body Language Techniques to Succeed   60
10. Ethical Principles in Business Practices   82
11. Career Action Plan   85
12. Develop Advanced Communication Skills   90
13. Guidelines for a Group Discussion   96
14. Develop a Corporate Image   101
15. Cultivate Practical Management Wisdom   104
16. Build Global Networking Skills   108
17. Develop a Risk Management Plan   115

■ Contents

18. Dealing with Stress	119
19. Team Building in the Workplace	126
20. Strategies to Resolve Conflict	130
References	*135*

Special Thanks to...

Daniel Goleman, *Author - Emotional Intelligence: "Why It Can Matter More Than IQ"*

I am grateful to Daniel Golemen, for the permission to reference his breakthrough concept of Emotional Intelligence in this book.

Gretchen Rubin, *Author - The Happiness Project/Better than Before*

Thank you for granting me permission, to include your thought-provoking ideas on habits, happiness and human nature.

Dr. Martin E.P. Seligman, – A special word of gratitude to Dr. Martin E.P. Seligman, for the outstanding support with the **Seligman Attributional Style Questionnaire(SASQ)**, the unique testing method for Emotional Intelligence.

David Calver, - I wish to express, a sincere thank you to David Calver, editor and proof reader for the diligence, and extra effort to make my book the best it can be.

Testimonial

The author combines her knowledge from what she has learnt in a very practical approach to Human Resource principles that can be applied in day-to-day situations. This book will help professionals succeed in today's competitive recruitment market, develop a better work-life balance and secure their ideal goals.

– **Rodney Barretto,**
Senior Director, Supply Chain Management.
Inventory Portal
Houston, Texas, USA

Author's Preview

I wrote this book with the desire to make a profound contribution to the professional success of every person, eager to fulfill their respective goals and desires. It will empower the reader, and draw attention to the simplest, yet most powerful tools to develop employment and management wisdom. The work includes a broad and integrated approach to people and organizational sustainability. The study and illustrations create the foundation for a global career.

The book offers to the reader's a first-hand experience to develop an international career. The goal is to help the reader build a long-term career strategy, enhance interview skills and develop communication proficiency. It functions as a complete employment guide through the various stages of career development and professional excellence in a highly competitive job market.

– Serina Sidhu

About the Author

Serina Sidhu, a Human Resources Management professional, educated and trained in Canada, has progressive international work experience from leading multinational companies, including Safeway, a top American retail chain and TELUS Canada, a global leader in telecommunications.

Formerly, as a Managing Partner of an Arts and Novelty Company, she has over ten years of extensive experience from Product Management to Marketing Strategy to International Business development across India and the USA.

An Alumna of Georgian College of Applied Arts, and Technology, Barrie, ON, Canada, Serina, has completed Post-Graduate studies in Human Resources Management with honors. Before pursuing higher education in Canada, she has earned a Master's Degree in English Literature from India.

Serina held the position of the Board of Director of North Eastern Centre of Community Society, in the city of Calgary, Alberta, Canada in the year 2010. In addition, she contributed extensively to community development as a Board of Director for the Taradale Community Association in Calgary, Alberta, Canada.

A member of the Writers International Network, Vancouver, B.C., Canada, she has chaired a number of seminars and held regular workshops for the United Way of Calgary, to address the early settlement issues of new immigrants including communication and language skills training, cultural integration and labour market research.

Serina specializes in interview skills, image management and cultural diversity. She can provide training on leadership, stress management, business communications, résumés and cover letters.

As soon as Serina decided to go overseas for higher studies, her father was detected with Cancer, he died within six months, keeping her resolution firm, she continued with her plan to pursue higher education in Canada, after the completion of the course, she returned to India to live with her mother. She lost her while writing this book. A keen golfer, she draws enormous inspiration from the words of golf legend Jack Nicklaus, widely regarded as the greatest

■ About the Author

professional golfer of all time: "Resolve never to quit, never to give up, no matter what the situation."

If you would like to have Serina to come and speak to your institution or organization, or if you would like to send your thoughts and comments please email at sdh_srn@yahoo.ca.

For more information, please visit www.serinasidhu.com

Acknowledgement

My heartfelt appreciation goes to Rodney Berretto, Senior Director, Supply Chain Management, Inventory Portal, Houston, Texas, for the wonderful testimonial written by him.

Ms. Ruthaane Krant, Co-ordinator of the Human Resources Management program, Georgian College of Applied Arts and Technology, Barrie, ON, Canada who motivates me in countless ways, and to all my teachers of the HRM program for their dedication, teaching excellence and contribution towards my education and learning. Ms. Gabe Turner Preston, my supervisor in Telus Communication, Calgary, Canada for her constant support and encouragement. The Directors of Jurisconsultus, for providing me with excellent support. Ondrej Palat, Lawyer, Prague, Czech Republic, who talked things over and offered his comments about the book.

I owe a huge thanks to Air Commodore and Mrs. G.S. Cheema, for always making me smile with their motivation. Colonel Jaswant Sandhu, for his insight and encouragement to achieve this goal. Ms. Manisha Mohan, Senior Vice-President, Design and Animation, Tata Interactive Systems, Mumbai, who has been with me through the years as a friend and well-wisher. Mrs. Lakhwinder Dhillon, Head of Department, Public Administration and Associate Professor, Sri Guru Gobind Singh College, Chandigarh, for her good thoughts and never-failing encouragement. Dalbir Thind and Manvinder Thind for their unfailing support.

A special word of appreciation for renowned artist Ms. Kannu Kanwaljeet; without her artistic excellence and outstanding contribution this book would not have been complete.

Last, not the least to my family, friends and well wishers, who saw me through this book-writing initiative. I'm grateful for all the support and hope the readers find this book useful!

Chapter 1

Find The Perfect Job

"Keep your dreams alive. Understand to achieve anything requires faith and belief in yourself, vision, hard work, determination, and dedication. Remember all things are possible for those who believe."

– GAIL DEVERS

A job search is an initiative to first find employment and keep going until you find the right career opportunity. There is nothing beyond reach. A positive mental attitude will help you maintain a strong belief in yourself. Organize your professional growth, identify undesirable traits and cultivate desirable qualities.

George, a senior business leader with a well-defined career map and a steady job growth, was out of work because of sudden downsizing by his company. He used the break as a chance to carefully examine his day-to-day failures and shortcomings. In a short time, he got hired by a much larger organization with a bigger salary package and extraordinary benefits. In the words of George, "Adversity has been my greatest teacher; facing uncertainly, and helplessness gave me a far greater understanding of my strengths, weaknesses, and an opportunity to redefine my long-term goals, and objectives."

Whether you are looking for internship, or a full time job or an alternate career, committing to your goals, will lead you to getting selected for a job interview, which may ultimately lead to your primary purpose of getting hired.

An intelligent and progressive plan significantly rewards a job search. Consistent and unfailing effort creates trust. Stepping out of your comfort zone by marketing your skills and accomplishments can give you the advantage of being noticed by more employers, and keep up with the fast pace of the changing global workforce.

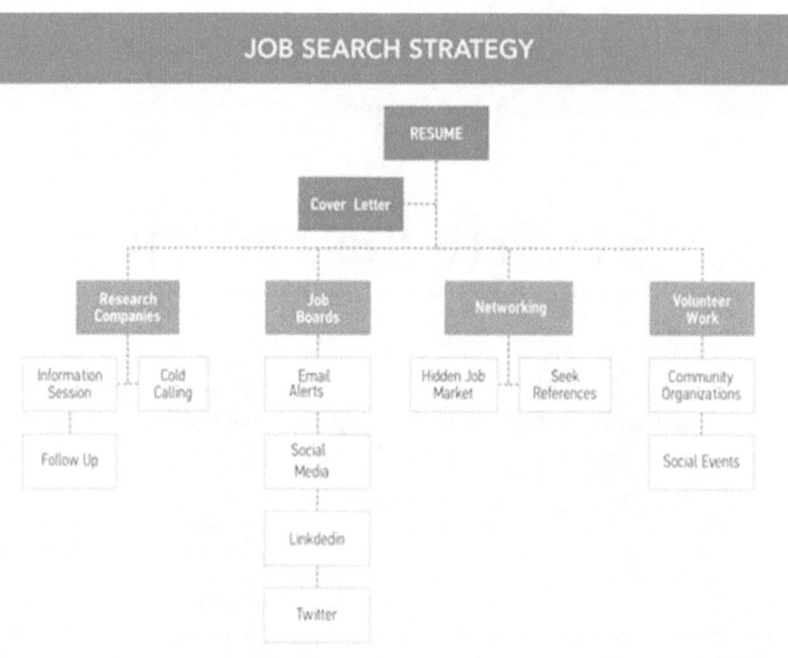

Effective Ways to Find Employment

A job search needs to be conducted in a well-planned and systematic manner. The traditional method of sending out a résumé in response to job advertisements still works, but is no longer the only way of finding work. Exploring job opportunities has been moving more online since the year 2008. From the very start, maintain a detailed record of the jobs applied to, contacts and the feedbacks received from potential employers.

Résumé Writing

A résumé has to be written in a specific format. Each layout serves a particular purpose. Be sure to choose the correct format and keep your résumé updated.

Cover Letter

The first thing a potential employee sees is the cover letter. Written in the form of a business letter, it must be sent along with every résumé.

References

The present global hiring trend is based on references. Nearly 70% to 80% of jobs are not advertised. Other than being a low-risk option for employers, hiring managers prefer candidates who are able to provide valuable references. Internal references refer to co-workers, supervisors, and managers. External references include friends, family, and community organizations. Through references, employers choose from 10 résumés to interview candidates, as compared to 219 from job advertisements.

Networking

Networking skills will help you develop a valuable list of contacts. According to a recent survey, networking is the leading source for finding employment.

Research Companies

Conducting a thorough research of the company before a job interview gives the candidate an edge over others. To start with, the company's website is the best source to gain knowledge about the company. Make a note of the names of the leadership team, competitors, mission statement and the work culture.

Information Sessions

A positive and proactive step by the job seeker, displays a passion and, intense desire to seek employment. Typically, it is a short meeting between a potential candidate, and a member of the hiring team.

Hidden Job Market

The hidden job market refers to a process of internal hiring, where companies prefer to promote or reorganize their work force, from within their team of employees. The only way to break into the hidden job market is through professional or personal contacts within the company.

Job Boards

The job board remains, a mode of hiring by some companies. It is advisable to upload your résumé on some of the best job boards like Monster & Career Builder. Indeed.com allows you to search job boards, company career pages, associations, and other employment websites that list jobs. According to experts, your résumé should match 80 to 85 percent of what an employer asks for in the job description.

Social Media

Recruitment through social media has increased by 90%. Companies globally are investing more into recruiting through the internet. Based on their users and emphasis, the scope of each social media site is different. An online portfolio has to be built in the form of a traditional online résumé. Always keep your job and contact information updated.

Online Image

Employers are inclined to hire candidates, based on their searches in Google. Represent yourself extremely well online. An overall view of your personality, range of interests, and your communication skills are reflected through your online portfolio.

LinkedIn

URL: www.linkedin.com

Background: Used by close to 450 million professionals worldwide.

Facebook

URL: www.facebook.com

Background: Used by more than 1.70. billion users.

Twitter

URL: http://twitter.com

Background: 3.3 billion users are on Twitter each day.

Job Shadow

URL: www.jobshadow.com

Background: 75,000 or more visitors per month, used mostly by young working professionals and entrepreneurs.

Volunteer

Volunteering before taking up a job is one of the most effective ways to find employment. Important workplace skills, like team building, problem solving, project planning, and organizational management are best learned through volunteer work. In addition, it is a perfect solution to gain practical work experience in your field of work, without the pressure and demand of a full-time job. Preferably try to get experience in your profession, e. g. law students can volunteer in a law firm. Similarly, IT students should volunteer for a software company.

Hiring Trends

The hiring trends differ across industries. It is important to understand the in-depth needs of an organization. According to a senior lawyer from a leading law company, apart from legal knowledge, the primary skills they look for in interns is the ability to write drafts and legal documents.

Cold Calling

Every job seeker can benefit from cold calling to reach their dream company. Employers prefer candidates who take the initiative of directly approaching them. Although it will never be easy, with confidence, politeness, and persistence you can make things happen. This approach works more with start-up and mid-sized companies.

Perseverance

Sometimes, no matter how professional, polite, friendly, or considerate you are or how hard you have tried, you may not get the desired outcome. If this happens do not get disappointed. Find an alternate way to succeed. In the words of renowned American author Napoleon Hill, "The majority of men meet with failure because of their lack of persistence in creating a new plan to take the place of those which fail."

- Understand the needs of the employer.
- Employers change their preferences and behavior from time to time.
- Manage your online profiles and posts in a way that would not lead a perspective employer to reject you.
- A large majority of employers reject candidates based on a negative profile on Google.
- There is no fixed technique that works all the time; the rule of thumb is to be persistent, optimistic, and pay close attention to the needs of the employers.

Summary

1. Keep your résumé updated.
2. Print a personal business card.
3. Send emails to all personal and professional contacts for job opportunities, in their organizations, and for job references.
4. Proactively seek volunteer opportunities.
5. Identify job opportunities and monitor future employment trends.

Chapter 2

Pre-Interview Guidelines

"One important key to success is self-confidence. An important key to self-confidence is preparation."

- ARTHUR ASHE

A job interview, at its best, should be viewed as a conversation between two individuals who are attempting to get to know each other during a discussion. The employer will attempt to learn more about your skills, knowledge and experience, or if you have the work ethics they are looking for in an employee.

The golden rule to succeed in an interview is to keep your emotions under control. Never discuss your previous employer or people in bad light, instead, focus on your professional goals. Interviewers prefer candidates who are interested in bettering themselves. It's a quality that indicates you will be considered for the job and grow with the company.

The reason for your job change will be a point of discussion in any job interview. Plan your response and practice it aloud so that you're prepared in advance. You do not want to sound like someone who is willing to attempt a job change on the slightest pretext and more so solely for financial gains.

Stay up to date with the company's information. The easiest way to do this is to set up Google alerts for the company. Answer with focus, concentration and sincerity. Do not give the impression of holding back information.

■ The Empowered Employee

Culture and Reputation

Conduct a detailed research about the company. Gather information from their websites, newspaper reports, past employees, friends and family members.

In the case of a lesser-known company, do your due diligence of any improper conduct or practice by them. According to research the number one reason for failing in an interview, is the lack of research and understanding of the hiring company by the candidates.

Key Areas to Research

- Products/Services
- Company Hierarchy
- Annual Revenue
- Growth Plan
- Culture
- Competitors

Practice and Rehearse

Organize your thoughts in systematic a manner. Prepare for spontaneous responses. This will help you develop confidence and a sense of self belief.

According to Peter T McIntyre, Painter and Author, "Confidence comes from not always being right, but from not fearing to be wrong."

References

Most often, employers ask for references. Secure references of at least three important people – former colleagues, supervisors and instructors, who will be willing to act as professional references. Be sure to get their permission before the interview, and be certain that these individuals will speak well about you. During the interview, you can casually use the name of your reference, more so if the individual holds a prominent place in the industry.

Attitude

A large number of employers are realizing the mistake of hiring for the right skills, but the wrong attitude. They have begun to show preference for candidates with the right attitude: "Hire for Attitude and Train for Skills" is their motto. *According to Alan Davidson, an industrial psychologist from San Diego, whose clients include*

Chevron, Merrill Lynch and the Internal Revenue Service, *"The single best predictor of future behavior is past behavior."*

Portfolio

A portfolio is a visual representation of your past work. It not only showcases your accomplishments; it also gives you added value. Even though a portfolio may not be essential for all positions, putting together one will make you look professional, and be seen as someone who is hard working and willing to go the extra mile.

Privacy

Do not discuss any confidential information of your previous company. Sharing confidential information of your past job will immediately create a sense of mistrust in you.

Prepare and Plan

Plan your mode of travel and visit the location of the interview a day before the meeting. Keep the name and the phone number of the individual you are to meet handy.

Dress Code

Research indicates that interviewers form their opinion in the first 5 seconds of meeting the candidate, and most jobseekers do not present themselves well during the first few minutes of a job interview, leading to a failed outcome.

- Freshly laundered/washed, preferably dark coloured (Grey/Dark Blue) pant suit, white or cream full-sleeves shirt, and polished formal shoes for male candidates.
- Neatly groomed hair, trimmed nails, formal hair style for men, and well manicured nails for both men and women. A lady candidate can choose to apply nail paint in a neutral shade.
- Minimize the use of colognes and sprays. Employers are highly sensitive to the possibility of an allergic reaction to strong-smelling perfume and cologne.
- A portfolio or briefcase for men; a portfolio or formal handbag for women.
- Brushed and flossed teeth. Eliminate bad breath of food, drinks and cigarettes.

➢ In addition to these guidelines, make sure to review the cross cultural dress code. For example, in the state of Punjab in North of India, candidates are advised to wear a turban in one colour. The preferred colours are light yellow, maroon, royal blue and navy blue. The colour of the turban can match the shade of the tie. Avoid being dressed in a cap or a head covering like the *Patka* for an interview.

- Employers are primarily concerned about the risk of hiring the wrong candidate.
- The need of every employer for the same job is different.
- Focus on how an employer will benefit by hiring you.
- Visualize success in the interview.

Summary

1. *Start preparing for the interview by making points.*
2. *Make a list of references.*
3. *Practice and improve your speaking skills.*
4. *Prepare to handle the unexpected, i.e. cancellation of an interview, bad weather or an accident.*
5. *Book your tickets, make the hotel booking and arrive 24 hours before for an outstation interview.*

Chapter 3

Ace your interview

"Big jobs usually go to the men who prove their ability to outgrow small ones."

- RALPH WALDO EMERSON

The process of holding interviews in a global work environment has taken on a completely new meaning. The candidates are tested on a number of different skills. Interviewers use a set of different formats to test the skills and potential of a job applicant. Every prospective employer will want to know what makes you different from the other candidates.

To succeed, it is important to develop and demonstrate flexibility. The recent trend is to move full-time employees to part-time positions. Most employers look for employees who can handle this change.

How to Face an Interview

- The first twenty seconds can be intimidating for both the interviewer and the candidate.
- The greater the preparation, the better your chances of stepping out of the interview with a job.
- Identify the reason behind each question, and respond accordingly.
- The first fifteen seconds of an interview is crucial to convey the right impression to the interviewer. 60-80% of the impact is made through non-verbal communication.
- Maintain direct eye contact with a subtle expression. Do not stare.
- The golden rule is never to outshine or argue with the interviewer.
- Despite all your achievements, practice humility during the interview.

- Do not respond if you have not understood a question fully; politely request the interviewer to repeat it.
- Learn, and practice the skill to withdraw from the conversation at the right time.
- A timely, open-hearted and honest response will create a very positive impression, in the mind of the interviewer.
- The interviewer's main purpose is to recruit employees who are passionate about what they do.

Different Interview Formats

One-to-One Interview

A one-to-one job interview takes place between the job candidate and an interviewer. It is an in-depth interview where the interviewer is usually a person directly related to the job.

Group Interview

A group interview, also called a panel, board or team interview, includes a group of interviewers. Once the question has been asked, respond directly to the panellist who asked the question. During the entire interview make eye contact with every member of the panel. This interview type is mostly conducted during the second or third round, to better judge the suitability of the candidates.

Mealtime Interview

A candidate is closely observed for social skills and manners.

- **Dress Code: Formal**
- **Table Layout**
  - Start at the outside and work your way in. Your salad fork will be on the far left; your entree fork will be next to it. Your dessert spoon and fork will be above your plate.
  - Liquids are placed on the right side of the plate and solid food on the left. For example, your water glass will be on the right and your bread plate will be on the left.
  - Put your napkin on your lap once everyone is seated.
- **Course of the Meal**
  - Do not choose to order the most expensive dish on the menu.

- Avoid food with too much gravy, chicken with bones, ribs, big sandwiches, and large portion of meats and vegetables.
- Place an order for food items that are easy to cut into bite-sized pieces.
- The polite way to eat soup is to spoon it away from you.
- Break your dinner roll or bread/chapatis/naan into small pieces and eat it a piece at a time.
- If you need to leave the table, put your napkin on the seat or arm of your chair.
- After you have finished eating, place your knife and fork in the "four o'clock" position.
- During the meal, relax, listen and participate in the conversation.
- **After the Meal**
  - Put your napkin on the table next to your plate.
  - Let the prospective employer pick up the food bill. The person who invited is expected to pay both the bill and the tip.
  - Thank the interviewer for the meal.
  - Follow-up with a prompt thank-you note.

Stress Interview

The candidate is put in a stressful situation before being given the opportunity to respond. The main purpose of this interview is to analyze the strength, resilience, adaptability and patience of a potential employee to handle pressure, hostile and provocative behavior.

Informational Interview

Prepare questions before sending out a request for an informational interview. A potential employer may just surprise you with an unexpected phone call, to discuss your skills and contribution to the company.

Behavior Based Interview

This type of an interview tells the employer what is unique about the way you will perform on the job, based on the belief that the "past predicts the future". Demonstrate your skills and expertise on how you will handle a situation described by the interviewer.

Screening Interview

This interview is conducted where there are a large number of candidates. The main purpose of this interview type is to uncover whether you possess or lack the "basic skills" necessary for the job.

Skype Interview

An interview through Skype is a popular method of interviewing long-distance candidates during the early stage of the interview.

- Closely watch Skype interview session videos uploaded online.
- Conduct a practice interview with a friend or professional associate.
- Pay attention to your environment and lighting.
- Position yourself correctly before the camera.
- Look directly at the interviewer and smile.
- Use the highest speed internet connection option available.

Cross-Cultural Interview

A cross-cultural interview requires extra preparation. The meeting takes place between two people from different cultures.

To avoid any miscommunication, the primary objective should be to overcome the language barrier. The interviewer and interviewee must both be acquainted with each other's values and belief to be sensitive to the culture and background of the candidate. For a successful outcome the interviewer should make an unbiased assessment and avoid snap judgments. There is a need to adopt and practice more tact and patience as non-verbal communication will differ between the participants. A panel interview is usually more successful in comparison to a one-on-one meeting.

Multiple nationalities including Americans and Canadians are highly sensitive to personal questions being asked during an interview. In some countries including India, asking personal questions like age, marital status and personal interests is common in some interviews.

■ The Empowered Employee

Best Interview angle - 45°

"Seated in the 45-degree angle, takes pressure off the interview"

During an interview, A candidate who speaks less may be understood as someone who is trying to hide vital information about their past negative behavior or background. Ms. Sheryl Stella, US based HR Business Partner, supports the view that an interview should be based on the 80/20 Rule. The candidate should do 80 % of the talking, while the interviewer should contribute only 20% to the discussion, to identify if the candidate will fit the role.

A candidate is very closely watched. The slightest behavior and gesture is noticed to help determine how the individual would act within an organization. Research shows that the first **"15 seconds"** of an interview is crucial.

In a face-to-face interview, a pause can make you appear wise and measured with your responses.

Each employer keenly observes the personal habits, mannerisms, self-confidence, empathy and the integrity of a potential employee.

Common Interview Questions and Answers

Tell me about yourself?

Answer: A brief "Profile Summary" (two minutes maximum, preferably less) of your education, experience, skills and interests that match with the job.

What is your most memorable accomplishment?

Answer: Describe your accomplishments in the form of a short narrative. Highlight skills that relate to the position.

What are your professional goals, five years from now?

Answer: Describe short-term achievable goals, and how you see yourself achieving long- term goals, through on-the-job experience, continuing education and hard work.

What are your strengths?

Answer: Describe strengths relating to the position, other than these mention generic skills which are greatly appreciated by all employers, such as:

- How you handled a pressure situation?
- The willingness to do extra.
- The ability to learn quickly.
- Problem-solving skills.
- Team-building skills.
- Leadership skills.

What is your greatest weakness?

Balance a weakness with a compensating strength, such as:

Answer: "I have the tendency to accomplish a lot in less time. Even though this adds pressure, it helps me better my multitasking skills".

What is your definition of both success and failure?

Answer: Respond with examples of how, you balance success and failure in your work and day-to-day life. Discuss how you tend not to get carried away by success and how you have made it a practice to learn from past failures.

What does the word anxiety convey to you, and how do you overcome it?

Answer: Give examples of how you accept anxiety as a part of life. Describe how it makes you appreciate the happy events better.

Is there anything in particular you would like me to know about you?

Answer: Discuss your strong points that could contribute to the job, and why you are the best candidate for the job.

Why should I hire you over other candidates?

Answer: Select five key strengths which could make you an asset for the position. Highlight areas of specialized skills, applicable job skills, and unique personal qualities that show you as better than the other candidates.

What kind of experience do you have for this position?

Answer: Present specific examples of your skills in dealing with similar projects. Provide details of the scope of activity you handled, and the outcome you achieved. Most employers look to hire candidates who are true problem solvers.

In what way have you progressed since the start of your career?

Answer: Give details of the number of positions held, on-the job training, and how you have made an effort to continue your education to keep up with the growing change in technology, range of work and cultural diversity.

What are your career plans?

Answer: Give a realistic response of your long-term goals and objectives and state that the only way to get there is through constant effort, hard work and commitment.

Questions about the Job and Company

What do you know about this position?

Answer: Give a detailed description of your understanding of the job, and mention how your skills and contribution will help the company further its goals.

What do you know about our competitors in the industry?

Answer: Describe the current industry trend. You should be prepared with the information about the competitors. Give a suggestion on how the company you are interviewing for can gain an advantage over its competitors.

What in your opinion are the challenges facing our company?

Answer: Give a detailed response based on your research, and draw a long-term focus of where the company stands with regard to continuing changes taking place in the global environment.

What do you see as the direction of our company?

Answer: Focus on the long-term goals of the company, preferably with facts and figures.

How long do you think it will take you to make a valuable contribution to our company?

Answer: Give details of how you will apply your key skills as a worker, and go that extra mile and contribute to the organization's goals and objectives.

What inspired you to apply for this job, and this company in particular?

Answer: Provide simple, clear and concise reasons. Convey your sincere enthusiasm, and a high level of motivation to work for the company.

Are you familiar with our company's mission statement, and do you feel it matches with your career goals and objectives?

Answer: If you feel you match the company's mission statement, start your answer by saying you have the expertise to match the mission statement of the company, a strong work ethic and the desire to be part of something big and challenging.

How do you think your skills will help our company further its goals?

Answer: Give details of your previous accomplishments in a similar role. Highlight at least three of your skills that match the job.

Tell me about how you delegate job responsibility?

Answer: Describe how you would delegate job responsibility to each member in your team. Give examples on how you handle critical issues.

Questions About Your Education

How do you keep your skills updated with the emerging trends?

Answer: Give a factual and effective response with examples. At the very start of your career join professional groups, attend seminars, workshops, read journals, and participate in blogs discussing job trends and new topics.

Do you consider academic degrees important for job success? Give me an example?

Answer: State academic degrees are of importance, as they help turn your natural abilities into specialized skills. This gives you an edge over other candidates.

What are the courses which have helped you the most in your career development?

Answer: State the courses through which you feel your maximum learning took place, and helped shape your professional career.

There are a number of long-distance and online training programs, what in your view is the best way to gain value from them?

Answer: State that those online programs may not be too comprehensive, but are a convenient way to upgrade skills while being employed.

What are your interests, other than your job?

Answer: Develop interests that enhance physical and mental well-being, such as physical exercise orientated activities and intellectually stimulating games and hobbies.

Challenging Interview Questions and Answers

I see that you have frequently changed jobs, why is that?

Answer: Give a realistic response of your circumstances that have led you to change jobs frequently, be it project positions, company downsizing, or any unavoidable personal circumstance. State examples how each job transition has helped you gain diverse work experiences and learning.

Because you have been working in your last job for more than five years, do you feel you will have a hard time re-adjusting to a new company?

Answer: Give a realistic response. Accept that some previous work habits may slightly affect your initial performance. Reiterate that it will not be long before you adjust to the new work environment. Based on your past work experience you can add value and provide alternative insights on current business processes.

Why do you want to quit your present job?

Answer: Respond by saying that the present job does not lead you to your goals and that you seek a more challenging role. This attempt by you will give an opportunity to a more suitable candidate to get your job.

Have you ever been asked to resign?

Answer: If you have been asked to resign, say it with confidence that, it was a life-changing experience. It taught you how to handle stress, uncertainty and pressure.

Have you ever faced the challenge of being demoted?

Answer: Be honest about it. Say it was disappointing even when you did your best as an employee. On a positive note, this setback gave you the opportunity to introspect on your failures and shortcomings and accept change more readily.

Why have you had such a long gap in employment?

Answer: Explain any gap in employment with honesty, whatever the circumstances of not having been employed. Interviewers appreciate a truthful and straightforward response.

Post-Interview Questions and Answers

Ask intelligent and probing questions. Focus on the employer's business needs and requirements.

What does this job involve?

Answer: This question directly focuses on the job responsibilities and the demands associated with the position/role. It will convey a fair idea about the primary skills needed for the job.

What are the skills a top employee would have to have to be hired for the job?

Answer: Should the interviewer say that he gives value to those candidates with certain traits like precision, diligence, and discipline, you will get an idea about the expectations of the interviewer.

Who are my co-workers and the team I would be a part of?

Answer: You can ask this question to get an idea of your co-workers as well as your future supervisors. The expectations, the typical culture, and the idea about the overall feel of the work environment will be understood.

Whose responsibility is it to see that I get the training I need here?

Answer: This question will convey to the interviewer your interest in progress and further learning. Do not sound over-eager, as it may give the impression that you are only interested in joining the company to gain knowledge and move on to more lucrative jobs.

How would I be evaluated, how often, and by whom?

Answer: Asking the question about feedback conveys to the employer your interest in improving on your strengths and weaknesses.

What were the strengths and weaknesses of the previous people holding this position?

Answer: This will demonstrate your interest to focus on specific strengths and perform to your maximum potential.

May I meet the person I would be working for (if it is not you)?

Answer: Demonstrates your interest to work and build positive relationships in the workplace.

What significant change has the company gone through in the past five years?

Answer: This question will establish your deeper interest in the company.

What values are sacred to the company?

Answer: This question will demonstrate to the employer the importance you give to values and character.

What future changes is the company planning to make?

Answer: Demonstrates your optimism about the future and how you would like to shape and modify your skills to fit the role.

Who do you look at as your allies or competitors in business?

Answer: This will demonstrate that you do not ignore competition and have a natural competitive advantage.

Salary Negotiation

In salary negotiation, the key is to do it with confidence and based on facts, not on emotions. The essential thing to remember is to remain detached from the outcome. The refusal for your preferred salary may have nothing to do with you, but the company's budget, the implications of other employees or rules and regulations instead.

- Depends largely on whether it is your first job, career change or seeking better employment prospects in the same profession.
- Determine your earning potential for the position through salary surveys.
- Provide examples of your results to prove to the company your worth and contribution in your previous job.
- Cautiously evaluate your current financial needs and circumstances.
- Never lie about your previous salary. Experts are trained to recognize dishonest and unethical actions.
- Conducting a salary survey before the interview will help you convey the exact worth of your education, work experience, and accomplishments.
- Even though it is important to be flexible, it helps to push for a slightly higher salary. Negotiate for perks like benefits, bonuses and vacation pay. At the same time, do not appear greedy or like someone who is motivated only by money.

Closing a Job Interview

Closing the job interview in an appropriate manner can make a significant difference to the outcome of an interview.

- Maintain a balanced approach to make a lasting impression on the interviewer.
- Keep your emotions under control until the end of the interview.
- Thank the interviewer with a courteous handshake and a pleasant smile.

Closing Comments

Depending on the response of the interviewer, type of business and culture of the organization, you can choose the following lines to close the meeting.

1. Thank you for sharing information about the company and the job. I feel confident about making a valuable contribution to the specific position and towards the goals of the organizations. It was a pleasure to meet you.
2. Thank you for giving me the opportunity to discuss my skills and qualifications for the job. I wish to work in your company and have the opportunity to be a part of your team. When can I expect a response or may I call, email or text to know about your hiring decision?
3. I hope to be considered for the role as I identify with the long-term goals and objectives set by the members of the management team and value the culture of the company including the philanthropic ideas and humanitarian initiatives.
4. Thank you for letting me share details about my skills and experience and discuss my suitability for the role. I look forward to hearing from you or may I call, email or text you at a suitable time to know about your hiring decision?
5. I have always had the desire to work for a company which hires and values cross-cultural employees. The challenge of being part of a multi-cultural workforce greatly inspires me. I am sure my skills, experience and commitment will add value to the organization. I wish to support and participate in the corporate philanthropy initiatives including the fund-raising events and community development.

Post-Interview Follow-Up

The post-interview conduct of a candidate is as important as the interview. Other than your job qualification, this question draws attention to your personal and social skills.

Send out a well-written "Thank you" letter within 24 hours of the interview. Compose a formal letter, with no spellings or grammar mistakes. Select good quality white paper, for both the letter and envelope. Alternately, you can send a "Thank you" email within 24 hours of the interview.

Reinforce your interest in the job and company, but do not sound desperate. Convey a subtle reminder of your skills and accomplishments, and highlight that the job suits your long term career goals.

Even if you have not qualified for the job, send a thank-you note in the following words, "Thank you for the opportunity of interviewing with you, please do keep me in mind for future job openings where my skills will better fit the position". This approach will set you apart from all other candidates, and leave a positive impression in the mind of the interviewer.

Key Answers Interviewers Seek About the Candidate

➢ Are you a team player?
➢ How will you handle change?
➢ How motivated are you to learn and grow with the organization?
➢ Are you into the job only for the salary or compensation?
➢ Do your personal goals match with the organization's long-term objectives?

- Before an interview research and gather recent interviewing trends from Google.
- Watch videos on YouTube for recent interview trends.
- Watch videos on table manners and proper etiquettes.
- The first 15 seconds of an interview are vital. 60 – 80 percent of the impression is non-verbal.
- View recruitment videos for a day-to-day life of an employee in the company.
- Use the interviewer's name at the beginning, during and after the interview.
- Never say anything bad about your previous employer or peers.
- It is considered natural and important for a candidate to ask questions after the interview.
- A "Thank You Note" sent soon after the interview will correct any wrong impression the interviewer got during the interview.

■ The Empowered Employee

 *Summary*

1. Study the difference in the hiring trends between old and new companies.
2. Prepare answers to as many challenging questions as you can. This will help you gain confidence and be comfortable during the interview.
3. Practice for all interview types and formats.
4. Conduct an in-depth salary survey of the job.
5. Prepare to ask questions to the interviewer after the interview.

CHAPTER 4

DEVELOP STRONG LEADERSHIP SKILLS

"A leader is one who knows the way, goes the way and, shows the way."

– JOHN C. MAXWELL

An effective leader establishes a perfect co-relation between personal goals and the objectives of an organization. Other than the required skills and competences, high-performing leaders develop qualitative and quantitative strategies.

THE LEADERSHIP STRATEGY

GOAL
- Identify Goals
- Set Targets
- Assess Market Needs
- Stress on Quality

PLANNING
- Return on Equity
- Return on Investment
- Return on Sales
- Return on Net Profit

ACTION
- Decision Making
- Manage Resources
- Monitor Competitors
- Employee Retention

SKILLS AND ABILITIES
- Specialized Knowledge
- Anticipate Crisis
- Correct Timing
- Problem Solving
- Team Building
- Change Management

■ The Empowered Employee

Essential Qualities of Leadership

Lead

True leaders take the initiative of leading their team with a sense of purpose and direction. The ultimate power of a leader is to make people do as you wish. The truth is that anyone can lead, but very few can achieve excellence.

Inspire

People respect those who inspire them and motivate action. A competent and hard-working leader has the willingness and ability to make both happen. To improve performance, managers should speak to subordinates. Success is based on the cause and effect of a relationship. Boost performance by offering feedback and suggest guidelines on improving performance.

Vision

Forecasting an outcome beyond its immediate vision is the greatest ability of a remarkable leader. Co-founder and Chairman of Microsoft, Bill Gates, revolutionized the concept of leadership. The example of his ability to analyze, interpret and visualize success will rule the business world for decades.

Intuition

Intuitive decision-making is gaining acceptance in present leadership practices. Seen beyond a technical and analytical perspective, intuition takes place when the subconscious conveys thoughts and ideas without the need for conscious reasoning.

Defined in the words of Ralph Waldo Emerson, American essayist, lecturer, and poet, "The good news is that the moment you decide that what you know is more important than what you have been taught to believe, you will have shifted gears in your quest for abundance. Success comes from within, not from without."

Kindness

A leader must have the ability to understand and care. Sensing others' feelings is the most powerful tool of a successful leader. A manager with empathy lets his team express themselves freely. Your realness will make you accessible, and encourage people to like you. A leader who does not practice kindness is heading for failure.

In the words of renowned American talk show host, actress and philanthropist Oprah Winfrey, "Leadership is about empathy. It is about having the ability to relate to and connect with people for the purpose of inspiring and empowering their lives."

Delegate

To effectively operate an organization, it is essential to delegate responsibility and monitor output.

Reputation

A successful leader must have credibility and the skill to lead with principles. Steve Jobs, Co-founder, of Microsoft Inc, and CEO and Chairman of Apple Inc, developed one of the best practices of building a reputation based on honesty, hard work and respect.

Communication

Listening or being heard is an important aspect of leadership. When you listen carefully, you win people's trust. According to a recent study, the higher one goes, the greater the need for communication. It is impossible to preserve trust without open communication and direct talk.

Integrity

Ethical standards in leadership are qualities that include truthfulness, credibility and honesty. Integrity makes sure commitments are not broken. In the absence of this trait, coordination and collaborations suffer.

No real success is possible without fair and honest business dealings. Author and leadership expert John Maxwell titled his book "There's Is No Such Things as Business Ethics", which shocked many readers.

Maxwell explained that you either have ethics or you don't. There isn't one set of ethics for business and another for your personal life. There's simply ethics. There's simply integrity, truthfulness and reliability. About being upright, *Maxwell also said, "There are really only two important points when it comes to ethics. The first is a standard to follow. The second is the will to follow it."*

Reliability

Reliability involves building trust by following the highest level of integrity. Trusted leaders provide a sense of comfort to their subordinates. A leader, who can be trusted during all eventualities, boosts morale and gives a feeling of security to the workers.

One method to help increase your reliability is to enlist an accountability partner to give honest feedback. Choose someone you know closely, respect, trust and share a common perception in terms of attitude, values and ethics.

Gratitude

Honoring and nurturing a team is the hallmark of a great leader. Gratitude is a POWER tool to succeed. A sincere thank you is the simplest yet the most powerful word often ignored by leaders. I urge all leaders to often use the word "GRATITUDE" to keep your staff members motivated and happy.

In the words of Charles M. Schwab, "I consider my ability to arouse enthusiasm among men the greatest asset I possess. The way to develop the best that is in a man is by appreciation and encouragement."

Reward

The boss must frequently reward and recognize the accomplishments of his subordinates. Other than monetary rewards, giving staff public credit and praise for their contribution is essential. The simplest and most effective way is to send a company wide email acknowledging the positive contribution of the specific employee.

Data and Information

A competent leader has to have the ability to manage data and information with precision and accuracy. Effective data management requires a manager to follow and comply with policies. In the IT and digital age, leaders are expected to align their technology in such a way that employees can communicate from remote locations. Link large and critical data to one master file. Manage both structured and unstructured data. Make data secure and flexible.

Social Intelligence

Research shows that there is a large gap in performance and output between socially intelligent and unintelligent leaders. Socially intelligent leaders have the skill and ability to engage in meaningful conversations, freely exchange ideas and create a transparent work environment.

The 3 C's of Leadership

Ability to Change

A natural choice of modern-day businesses is to prefer a leader with the ability to adapt, function beyond personal limitations and have the wisdom to cope with every eventuality. Adapting to change is critical, to remain competitive and respond to new sources of competition is essential.

Accept Change

A truly unique quality is to have the flexibility and willingness to accept change. The dramatic shift in the economy has forced leaders to accept change and adopt new skills sets. The most accomplished leaders keep up with the constant change in their area of work.

Bring Change

Each year organizations across all sectors invest capital. A leader needs to have the unique ability to predict the unfolding circumstances. To move in the right direction, organizational change is necessary in terms of strategy, leadership and purpose. An organization that does not initiate change does not meet the expectations of its stakeholders.

■ The Empowered Employee

- Leadership is about purpose, and commitment to excellence.
- Implement change to improve the bottom-line.
- Gather all information to make informed decisions.
- Courage and boldness are two of the most important qualities for a leader to succeed.
- Develop intuitive abilities.
- Serve as a positive role model.
- Practice gratitude, honesty and empathy.

Summary

1. *Train yourself to handle power with precaution.*
2. *Practice self-awareness techniques.*
3. *As a manager, be accessible, to staff members and clients.*
4. *Recognize and reward the contribution of the "Star Performers".*
5. *Learn to overcome anger and frustration.*

Chapter 5

Write an effective résumé
A Résumé Speaks

"When I interview somebody, I look at their résumé to see what they have done, who they have worked with, and how many times they have got repeat work. Those are the kind of actors I want to hire."

– JOE PANTOLIANO

A well-written résumé with a cover letter is the first point of contact between an employee and the employer. You are the best person to write your own résumé.

The present work culture is about creating the right impact. The ability to write short résumés is preferred by most employers. The art of effective résumé writing is to give the reader, an honest and brief description of your skills, accomplishments and potential. Surveys show that it takes only eight to ten seconds for a skilled human resource professional to scan a résumé. Even though, writing a résumé is not easy and needs a lot of hard work, it is worth the effort. Writing you own résumé will give you a sense of confidence, and the ability to express yourself better during an interview.

To stand out, a résumé needs to be written in a professional manner. Focus carefully, on the language, display, structure and organization.

Highlight international education and work experience in a manner that will benefit the employer. Stress on leadership, problem-solving and communication skills. Candidates with international work experience are hired for overseas operations and to strengthen cross-cultural business partnerships.

Focus on the following personality traits and individual characteristics to draw the attention of the hiring manager.

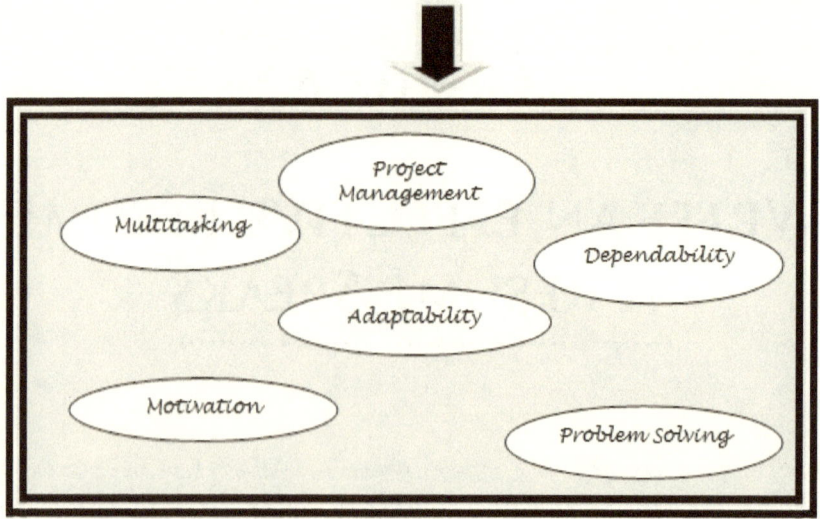

Difference Between Résumé and Curriculum Vitae

A Curriculum Vitae (CV), often referred to as an "academic résumé", is a detailed account of work experience, educational background, awards, honours, professional affiliations, publications, and research papers. In Europe, Africa, and Asia some employers may still expect to receive a Curriculum Vitae.

Essential Rules for Writing a Successful Résumé

Format

The first step to writing an effective résumé is to identify the correct résumé format based either on work experience, skills or education.

1. Chronological Style

This résumé is the most popular and easy-to-follow format for people with no break in employment. Start with your professional experience. Describe your most recent job and end with your first job.

2. Functional Style

This résumé focuses on skills. This format is suitable for students, for persons with long gaps in employment and less work experience.

3. Combined Style

This résumé style is a combination between the chronological and functional résumés. It is suitable for candidates who wish to make a career change or have less work experience.

Education

Start this segment with your highest level of education with dates. If you have a Master's degree, (Master's of Arts/Science/Commerce), add it before the Bachelor's degree, (Bachelor's of Art/Science/Commerce). If you are a recent graduate add your Score/Grade/GPA. Other than this any qualification relevant to the job you are seeking should be written after the Master's degree. In the absence of a Master's/Bachelor's degree include any education you have received.

Publication

Insert this subheading between your "Education" and "Work History" section. If you have more than five publications, choose your five most impressive titles. If your publications can make or break your chances of getting the job, list them on a separate page and attach that document to your application. Mention about the attachment in your cover letter.

Work Experience

The basic rule is to write all your past experiences in the past tense, and your current job in the present tense. It should be clear and easy to read. Include the following for each job:

- Name of the company or organization
- Job title
- Dates employed there
- Location – city and state
- Job responsibilities – *The general rule is to describe your job responsibilities and contribution in three to five bullet points.*

Responsibilities

- Trained 1000 sales team members on customer relations and monitored their performance.

Contribution
- Increased revenue by 12% in three months.

Summary
A summary statement is more preferred than an objective statement. A brief description of your experience, key strengths and achievements should be written in the beginning of the résumé.

Summary Statement - Example
"Dedicated and effective leader, able to prioritize, multitask and increase productivity in a fast-paced work environment. Adapts to change, maintains a positive attitude and strong work ethic. Recognizes excellence to build a high-performing team and overcome multicultural barriers through outstanding interpersonal relations."

Length
A two-page résumé format is preferred by most employers. Research papers and case studies should be sent along in the form of an attachment.

Language
Make use of professional language. Use attention-grabbing, action and dynamic words to create a mental picture. Abbreviations (e.g., etc., i.e.), technical jargon, slang or buzz words are strictly forbidden. Before sending the résumé make sure, there is no stain, line or crease on it. Do not use pronouns, (i.e., I, my, me, our, we, etc.).

Action Word/Verbs
The use of action words and verbs highlight a candidate's ability to lead, perform duties and meet deadlines.

Keywords (Search Engine Optimization)
The use of keywords to find a job online has made the job market competitive and strategic. Jobs are directly posted on the company websites. For example, search for a job by typing keywords specific to your career, skills, interests, company and place in Google. Some search engines may give you an estimate of the prevailing salary range for your job.

Fonts

The most popular and preferred font for a résumé is Times New Roman. It has been proved to generate more responses than any other font. For the text, a font size of 10, 11, and 12 is used; for more details use 10.5 or 11.5, not smaller than this. A font size of 14 to 16 is best for the name and address section.

Template

For best results, avoid the use of a readymade template. They include features which do not appear pleasing to the eye. Their layout is often complex, which may not suite your occupation.

Personal Details

Personal details include name, address, telephone/mobile number and email address.

Optional Information

In North America, no personal information or interests is shared in the résumé. In Asian countries like India, some employers prefer the employee to give details about age, marital status and religion.

Goals/Objective

Include a goal or an objective statement only if you are making a career change. Showing preference for a particular position can narrow and restrict your job search or you may get overlooked for a job which may perfectly match your skills and abilities.

Awards and Recognition

Service awards, recognitions, dean's list or any other honours and awards should be included in the Awards and Honours section.

Affiliations

Membership to an organization affiliated to your profession will help develop key contacts, and add more value to your résumé.

Volunteer Experience

Volunteer experience in a résumé conveys a positive and helpful attitude. It demonstrates the ability of the candidate to work with large groups of people. This is particularly useful for students and candidates with less work experience.

Foreign Languages

The ability to communicate in different languages makes it easier for an applicant to have an advantage over other candidates.

Self-Employment

Describe self-employment in the same manner as any other job experience. Highlight positive skills of creativity, self-discipline, financial acumen, ambition and drive that motivated you to start your own enterprise.

Frequent Job Change

Frequent job change has to be highlighted in a positive manner. Even though, your period of work was short, it has to show that you have contributed effectively to the organization and gained experience. A job change should not show that you have changed jobs due to monetary benefits, from being bored or lacking a goal to succeed.

Unemployment

Handling unemployment in a résumé is of extreme importance. Unemployment is one of the foremost concerns for most employers while screening candidates. A functional résumé format helps cover the gap in employment by drawing attention to your skills and abilities.

References

Do not mention the names of your references on your résumé. Make a list of the references on a separate sheet of paper. Seek their permission and a preferred time for a potential employer to contact them. Hand over the reference sheet after the interview, if requested by the interviewer.

LinkedIn

Employers will go to your LinkedIn profile to find more details about you.

Nearly 90% of employers check the online profiles of candidates. Include the link of your personal LinkedIn URL in the contacts section of your résumé. This will make it easier for the employer to identify your profile.

Email

Sending a résumé by email is the simplest, but not the best option, you need to do it the right way. There is always the possibility of it going to the spam folder or the security system of a company may block the email. Many employers may not open an attachment from an unfamiliar id.

Although, expert's views differ, one view is to paste it in the e-mail body along with an introduction of a few lines (40-60 words), and a professional subject line. The best method is to take the initiative and call the company to find out what they prefer.

Proofreading

Proofread the résumé for spelling and grammar mistakes. Then get at least two to three people to review and edit it, before you send it to a potential employer.

Layout

A simple layout is preferred by employers, unless your job involves the need to show graphics and design.

Spacing

Use single spacing with a blank line in between each section of the contents.

Margin

Margins range between .5 and 1 inch.

Paper and Printing

Black font on an A4-size white paper should be used to print the résumé. Never send a photocopy, always present a printed version only.

Bold Print

Bold prints are heavy on the eye and make a résumé hard to read. Use it only for your name and sub-headings.

Italics

Italics break the consistency of a document like the résumé. They should be used sparingly, for example, to highlight the names of journals or newspapers.

Capital Letter

The use of capital letters in the text of a résumé should be used with caution. Limit the use to the beginning of a sentence and after a full stop.

■ The Empowered Employee

Underlining

Avoid the temptation of underlining words in a résumé. Even though your intention may be to draw the attention of the reader to a particular position or skill, it is not well accepted by most employers.

Action Words

Addressed	Estimated	Proposed
Administered	Encouraged	Publicized
Analyzed	Ensured	Presented
Authorized	Expedited	Published
Allocated	Evaluated	Pursued
Arranged	Facilitated	Participated
Balanced	Focused	Recruited
Budgeted	Formulated	Reinforced
Collaborated	Filed	Referred
Communicated	Founded	Represented
Corresponded	Guided	Restructured
Calculated	Generated	Revised
Conserved	Gathered	Specified
Coached	Hosted	Suggested
Collaborated	Identified	Safeguarded
Consolidated	Influenced	Secured
Coordinated	Interviewed	Spearheaded
Compiled	Involved	Standardized
Discussed	Launched	Structured
Drafted	Maintained	Suggested
Designed	Managed	Supervised
Developed	Monitored	Targeted
Diagnosed	Maximized	Taught
Distributed	Motivated	Tested

Delegated	Negotiated	Trained
Directed	Observed	Transcended
Displayed	Obtained	Unified
Defined	Operated	Upgraded
Discussed	Organized	Utilized
Edited	Originated	Validated
Explained	Overhauled	Wrote

Targeted Résumé

A targeted résumé involves that extra effort of customizing the résumé to a specific job and company. It conveys the initiative and interest of an employee to work for a specific organization.

Non-Traditional Résumé

A non-traditional résumé is a web based résumé, similar to an online profile. It can include graphs and images.

Video Résumé

A video résumé is now being used by companies to short list applicants. Lasting for about 60 seconds, it gives the employer a clear picture of the personality and public speaking skills of a candidate. Present yourself in a professional manner. Dress in formal clothes. Speak about your experience, skills, education, strengths and passion. Make sure the camera and other equipment are of high quality. Look directly into the camera. A well-made video résumé can make a job applicant stand out.

■ The Empowered Employee

CATHERINE K MARAIS
SALES AND MARKETING PROFESSIONAL

Result-driven sales professional with over ten years of marketing and management experience, in-depth understanding of brand management and market analysis, expertise in identifying opportunities and establish long-term customer relationships.

AREA OF EXPERTISE
- Brand Management
- Customer Demand
- Market Analysis
- Market Progress
- Customer Relationship

WORK EXPERIENCE

Manager, Sales and Marketing — 2009 - Present
Idelle Clothing, Castle, CA

- Train and manage 40 staff members.
- Increase of the sales margin of High End Brands by 75%.
- Enhance customer base by 90%.
- Design and implementation of customer retention strategies.

Assistant Manager Sales — 2005 – 2009
Maazee Apparels, Castle, CA

- Evaluate style, quality and prices of competitor brands.
- Maintain in-store compliance of safety and security standards.
- Increase on average sales by 10% per day.
- Maintain a 75% repeat customer base.

ACADEMIC QUALIFICATION

Masters of Business Administration (Honors) — 2003 – 2005
Admin College, Castle, CA

VOLUNTEER EXPERIENCE
Child Care and Humanitarian Relief Society, Castle Town, CA

SOFTWARE/SYSEMT SKILLS
Window, Visual Basics, Access, HTML, Netscape/Internet Explorer

ADDITONAL SKILLS
English (read, write, and speak) French (speak)

Contact

Address
41, Maple Leaf Road, Castle, CA 00045-00045

Telephone
000.888.0000

Fax
000.999.9999

Email
Catherine.marais@domainname.com

Linkedin
url

Twitter

MARK ALFRED

Contact

Address
24, Prince Drive,
Horseshoe Land - CA.
00002-00002

Telephone
(777) 292-7879

Email
mark.alfred@domainname

 **LinkedIn**
Url

 Twitter

ENTRY-LEVEL SOFTWARE ENGINEER

In-depth knowledge and understanding of software packages and operating systems, ability to quickly learn new concepts and technologies, strong team leader with extensive background in managing and training junior students.

AREA OF EXPERTISE

- Database Management Systems
- Information Security
- Software Quality Testing
- Assembly Language Programming
- Software Engineering Process Management
- Networking Security

EDUCATION

Bachelors of Science in Information Technology   2007 - 2011
ON College of Information and Technology, Horseshoe Land, CA

WORK EXPERIENCE

Own- Communications, Horseshoe Land, CA   2011- Present

- Provide networking and desktop support to students and faculty members.
- Continuous improvement of new products by identifying and implementing positive changes.
- Develops understanding of and relation with internal and outsourced partners for new product introduction.
- Participates as a member of project team to develop and execute reliable, cost-effective and high-quality new products and solutions.

VOLUNTEER EXPERIENCE

Helping children with learning disabilities - Special Needs Organization, Horseshoe Land, CA

LANGUAGE PROFICENCY

English (Read, Write, Speak), Spanish (Read, Write, Speak), French (Speak).

GEORGINA M WILLIAMS
HUMAN RESOURCES GENERALIST

Maintained and managed benefits for over 5000 employees. Conducted training programs for 500 employees every week, handled employee safety and welfare, undertook compliance checks, regulatory control and report complaints to management.

SKILLS AND ABILITES
- Resourcing and planning
- Organizational Design
- Employee Contracts
- Learning and Development
- Reference Checks
- Employee Engagement
- Performance and Reward

EDUCATION

Post-Graduate in Human Resources Management   2005 - 2007
Academeez University, Castle, CA

Bachelors in Business and Economics   2002 - 2005
Proficient College of Management, Castle, CA

EXPERIENCE

Assistant Manager, Human Resources   2011 – Present
Hyireez, Castle, CA

- Assist in reorganizing the compensation structure of 5000 employees.
- Handle high volume of complaints and report to management.
- Coordinate weekly training programs for 500 staff members.
- Facilitate and monitor companywide health and safety measures.

Human Resources Administrator   2007 - 2011
Recomp, Castle, CA

- Prepare employee contracts and conduct reference checks.
- Handle new hires, personal information, salary package and benefits.
- Prepare job descriptions and competency appraisals.

VOLUNTEER EXPERIENCE
Board Member, Leadership and Community Society, Castle, CA

TECHNICAL EXPERIENCE
MAC-OS, Windows, Word, Excel, Power Point, Explorer, SAP, Oracle, Access.

Contact

 Address
11, Focal Street, Castle, CA 00001-00001

 Telephone
123-456-3126

 Fax
321-567-0909

 Email
georgina.williams@domain.com

 Linkedin
url

 Twitter

- A résumé should be written with a specific purpose; its main role is to get you invited for an interview.
- Do not mention the names of references on your résumé.
- Appropriate use of "Action Words" is important.
- A résumé should always be customized to the job and employer.
- Do not take it personally if an employer does not acknowledge receipt of your résumé; approximately only 45% respond, and 55% do not reply.

Summary

1. Identify the résumé format best suited for your job.
2. Develop the skill to write an effective résumé by following all the "rules."
3. Proofread the résumé five times before forwarding it to a professional résumé expert.
4. Clearly understand the difference between a curriculum vitae and résumé.
5. Practice to choose the right words to describe your skills and experiences.

Chapter 6

Create A Professional Cover Letter

"The résumé focuses on you past and the present. The cover letter focuses on the employer and the future. Tell the hiring professional what you can do to benefit the organization in the future."

– JOYCE LAIN KENNEDY

The cover letter is form of introduction attached to every résumé sent to a potential employer. Every résumé should be sent along with a cover letter. A recent survey has revealed that some employers prefer a well-written cover letter over a résumé.

Studies show that 80% of employers prefer to receive a cover letter with the résumé – and 30% will reject a résumé sent without one.

Presently, most employers prefer an online format sent via email, which can be read on smartphones and iPads.

Before sending the résumé, call the specific company and ask them about the format of the cover letter they prefer.

Focus on your skills, accomplishments and the desire to work in the organization. An individualized, motivational, thoughtful and persuasive cover letter prompts the employer to consider the applicant for an interview.

Cover Letter

The cover letter should be written on one page only. Divide the information into 3 – 4 paragraphs. Ensure that the cover letter is typed on superior quality white paper only. Never send a hand-written cover letter.

Heading: Cover letters use standard business style, with the sender's and the recipient's contact information.

Introduction: The introduction should briefly state your interest in the job and express your sincere desire to work in the organization.

Body: This typically includes the skills, qualifications and work experience of the candidate. Specific information, such as availability date, should be included in this section.

Closing: A closing sums up the letter and indicates the next step the applicant expects to take. It may indicate that the applicant intends to contact the employer. Many candidates adopt a more indirect approach and write "I look forward to hearing from you".

Ending: The ending is done with a (Sincerely) and (Signature). The abbreviated version of Enclosure (Encl) may be added.

Types of Cover Letters

E-Note

The e-note is now being preferred by most employers. Written in half the space of a traditional cover letter, it should be brief and concise. Include key skills, brief details of your work experience and the desire to work for the company.

Targeted Cover Letter

A targeted cover letter is written keeping a particular position in mind. It is important to write details about your skills and qualifications that match with the job description to convey to the company that you are a good fit for the job.

Cold Contact Cover Letter

A cold contact cover letter is written as a letter of introduction of your skills and professional experiences without any specific position in mind. It states the desire of the candidate to work for a particular organization.

Customized Cover Letter

A cover letter is addressed to the hiring manager for a career change, a specific job position or to request a salary increase.

Internship Cover Letter

When you're writing a cover letter for a summer job or internship, it should reflect why you are qualified and interested in the position. It's also a good idea to mention your availability, if the job posting mentions a start and end date for the job.

Cover Letter Applying for More than One Job

Highlight professional experience, skills and accomplishments. Customize it to each position within the same organization.

Job Promotion

An employee who is being considered for a job promotion may have to write an application, similar to a cover letter, to apply for the new position. The letter should explain in clear words the employee's qualification, skills and experience within the company.

Job Transfer Cover Letter

The applicant needs to mention the position and the location of the department they are seeking.

Request a Meeting

This is written by potential employees to request a meeting with a concerned official within an organization, to discuss their education, skills and experience. It can be written with reference to a specific position.

Cover Letter for Unadvertised Position

A cover letter for unadvertised position is also called a cold calling cover letter. It is addressed to the hiring manager of a specific organization to be considered for an interview for potential job openings.

Employee Referral Cover Letter

An employee referral cover letter is written when a candidate is referred for the position by a contact or an employee from within the organization.

Networking Cover Letter

This helps a potential employee reach out directly to an employer. It may include referral letters, letters of introduction and networking outreach letters.

Email Cover Letter

An email cover letter is written in the format of a traditional cover letter with two- to three-lines paragraphs marked by bullet points. Send the résumé in the form of an attachment. Insert the job title in the subject line. Include details about your following online profiles, including:

- LinkedIn URL.
- Twitter Handle.
- Professional Blog.
- Online Portfolio.
- Social Media Résumé.

Cover Letter Writing Tips

Select a Cover Letter

There are several forms of cover letters that can be sent to potential employers or contacts. Choose a format that clearly reflects your purpose and the assistance you are seeking.

Format a Cover Letter

How you format your cover letter, both the content (information) and presentation is equally important. Even when applying online or through email, the cover letter should look professional.

Review Cover Letter Examples

A cover letter template can be a good guide to write your first few cover letters. Using a cover letter template, will eventually help you develop your cover letter.

Include Key Words

Include words like wrote, analyzed, quantified, planned, programmed, designed, created, built, taught and trained to describe your work experience and skills.

Write a Personalized Cover Letter

A personalized cover letter should be addressed to a specific person in the organization. Write it in the form of a formal cover letter only. The use of jargon, slang, personal overtones or any other form of intimidation is strictly forbidden. Also research the company and its policy before sending it.

Explain Gap in Employment

A gap in employment, whether from being laid-off, out of work, taking time out for family commitments, going back to school, or for any purpose, should be explained with clarity and precision.

Sample Cover Letter

In the wide range of cover letters, the following is the sample of a cover letter sent along with a Resume.

Richard Jacob
21, Maryville Avenue
New York 10007

Gerald Green
Vice President
3 Deming Solutions
1214, Corporate Building
🏠 New York 10007
📞 (216) 000-0000
✉ richardjones@domain.com

12th January 2014

Dear Mr. Green,

I wish you a good day.

I am eager to work for, 3 Deming Solutions, a company known for its outstanding reputation and exceptional work ethics.

The position advertised by your company for General Manager, office operations in the Times Mail, suits my current education and skill sets, which I believe can add value to your organization. My experience so far has enabled me to take on responsibilities both in an office environment and within back-end operations. As a thorough working professional I am self-motivated, work hard and fit easily into any team.

Please find attached a copy of my résumé for your information and review.

I will follow up next Wednesday to learn about the possibility of being interviewed.

You can contact me anytime on (216) 000-000 or email me at richardjacob@domain.com

Yours Sincerely,

Richard Jacob

Cover Letter Mistakes to Avoid

Proofreading

After using an electronic grammar and spell check tool, place a finger on each word, read the letter out loud, correct the mistakes, read it again. Ask a friend or professional associate to review it.

Generic Cover Letter

The most common mistake candidates commit is to send similar cover letters to a number of employers. The right thing to do is to tailor your experience and skills to the job description.

Facts and Figures

Include facts, figures and statistics. Use bullet points to highlight them. They provide specific details about achievements and effectiveness. Attention to detail is needed.

Greetings

Make the effort to get the name of the hiring manager. Address the person by their first name and last name (e.g. Ms. Tiffany Brown); the use of "To Whom It May Concern" is completely forbidden. Dear Sir or Madam is no longer preferred. Instead you may use, Dear Hiring Manager. Address a lady as Ms. Simon and not Mrs. Simon.

Details

Sending a letter which is too short can send the wrong signal to employers about your level of interest in the job. You must convey your skills and abilities in the form of a well-written summary.

A lengthy cover letter can burden the reader, and the hiring team may move right to the résumé. The same can be said for paragraphs which are too detailed. Write 3 to 5 paragraphs with approximately 6 lines in each paragraph.

Specific Examples

Expressing empty opinions about your strengths will generally not convince an employer about you being suitable for the job. Quote specific examples of a job or role where you successfully employed those skills. Instead of stating, "I possess strong writing skills and an outstanding work ethic" write "Strong writing skills enabled me to revise a grant proposal and secure $100,000 in additional funding from the Jones Foundation".

Express Interest

Don't leave the hiring manager wondering about your level of interest. Express a genuine desire and interest in the job.

- Other than your skills and accomplishments, a cover letter should reflect your personality.
- Do not use words that express humor. This will convey a lighthearted approach.
- If you question the appropriateness of a sentence, trust your instincts and rewrite it.
- Express your enthusiasm without false praise or adulation.

Summary

1. Practice writing different types of cover letters.
2. A cover letter should be written as a brief introduction of your education, skills and work experience relevant to the job.
3. Write the cover letter based on the job description and express your interest in the job.
4. Learn to write an easy-to-read yet powerful and persuasive cover letter.
5. Recheck the correct date, month, company name, job title, name and designation of the person in the organization to whom you are addressing the cover letter.

CHAPTER 7

BUILD A POSITIVE MENTAL ATTITUDE

....

"If you don't like something, change it. If you can't change it, change your attitude."

– MAYA ANGELOU

FACTORS THAT IMPACT ATTITUDE

- INTELLIGENCE
- CORE VALUES
- THINKING
- EXPERIENCE
- ENVIRONMENT

'Keep your face always toward the sunshine - and shadows will fall behind you.'

– Walt Whitman

Intelligence

Intelligence primarily influences the attitude of a person. It impacts the opinion of a person based on education, beliefs, experience and environment.

Stages of Intellectual Development

1. Intelligence lays the foundation of thought, attitude, emotions, and associations. This first stage starts from childhood. During this period most education comes from external sources, such as parents, family, and teachers. The lack of learning and education during this time can lead to personality disorder of any type.
2. The second stage starts from adolescence to adulthood. This is the phase in life when the foundation is built to overcome challenges, and face the harsh realities of life. This is a stage of day-to-day survival.
3. The stage of life from 40 – 75 years is when most failures and successes are experienced.

Core Values

Values define you as a person. Your self-image is communicated by the values you follow. A lack of values destroys the potential for growth and improvement. Good habits help to develop harmonious relationships with others. Strong values also give an added advantage to accept and work positively around change and overcome adversities.

Thinking

Thought or thinking is the most powerful aspect that affects an individual's attitude. It helps build skills for success and controls the mind to block negative emotions. In recent years, researchers have found thoughts to have a powerful effect on the health and well-being of a person. A positive thought protects against depression and other personality disorders. This gives happiness and long-term success.

Experience

The impact of personal experiences, occurrences and circumstances has a strong impact on attitude.

Environment

External conditions impact an individual's attitude. The indirect actions of others can have a major impact on a person's attitude. The sense of fear, love, guilt, shame, discouragement, persistence, and courtesy are influenced by external factors.

"Experience is the best teacher, and the worst experiences teach the best lessons."

– ANONYMOUS

- Despite opposition, persist to achieve your goals.
- Take anticipatory action to avoid problems.
- Create opportunities and strive to do better and better.
- Positive feelings have a greater impact than negative thoughts.
- Overcome rejections, and work with principles and values.

Summary

1. Practice to control negative thoughts, and reactions.
2. Overcome arrogance, laziness, dishonesty and a lack of enthusiasm.
3. Seek the company of positive people.
4. Develop self-confidence. Believe in your skills and abilities.
5. Read positive and motivational books.

Chapter 8

Emotional Intelligence (EQ)

"In the last decade or so, science has discovered a tremendous amount about the role emotions play in our lives. Researchers have found that even more than IQ, your emotional awareness and abilities to handle feelings will determine your success and happiness in all walks of life, including work and family relationships."

– JOHN GOTTMAN

In simple words, Emotional Intelligence (EQ) is a person's ability to identify, assess, and control feelings. The good news is that, it can be learnt with practice.

The concept of emotional intelligence gained popularity after the publication of psychologist and New York Times science writer Daniel Goldman's book *Emotional Intelligence: Why It Can Matter More Than IQ*.

Emotional intelligence helps to develop core values and build new skills. Employers are laying great emphasis on a potential candidate's ability to create the right balance between knowledge, respect, courage, faith, and confidence.

Successful leaders appreciate individuals who display the ability to handle emotionally challenging situations. During an interview, close to 90% of this attribute sets candidates apart from, other job applicants. This factor helps employers judge and measure the ability of a candidate to manage others, develop new skills, and enhance productivity.

A lack of emotional intelligence comes in the way of taking correct decisions, a sign of serious incompetence. Such people can be easily pressured or intimidated. Overly sensitive to criticism, they are inclined to remain indifferent towards new ideas, approaches and information.

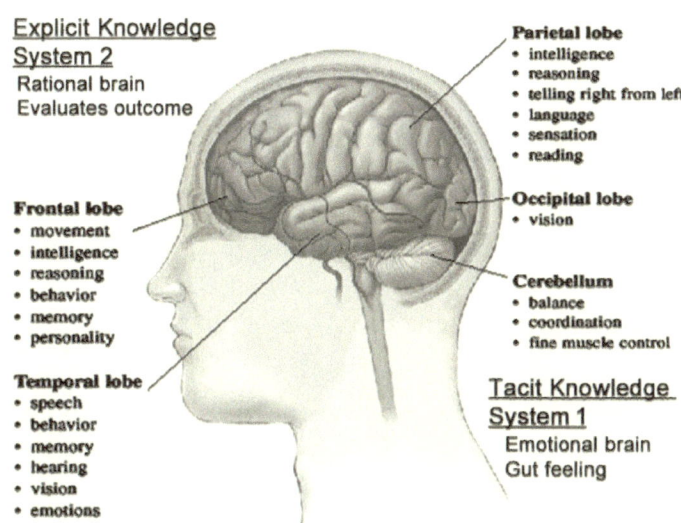

Self Awareness - Self Regulation - Motivation - Empathy - Social Skills

Method to Measure Emotional Intelligence

The Seligman Attributional Style Questionnaire (SASQ) is a unique method to test emotional intelligence designed by Dr. Martin E.P. Seligman after rigorous research of over 30 years. He is currently Professor of Psychology in the Department of Psychology at the University of Pennsylvania.

There is a definite co-relation between optimism and emotional intelligence. Optimists are in control of their lives. Across various industries optimists are rewarded for their decision-making skills.

The test reveals if a person will get defeated by circumstances or will fight back to achieve success. The SASQ is an extremely effective method to help employers select the right employees by recognizing their strengths and weaknesses. This decreases employee turnover.

The way a person describes their life experiences is a good indicator of their future behavior. Candidates with a positive attitude are more likely to transform adversities into accomplishments. Those who blame circumstances or even destiny are less likely to succeed.

The SASQ is available online. It is easy to understand and takes about 20 minutes to complete. It is designed to give accurate results. No one can manipulate or influence the scores. The online test makes it accessible to employers and potential employees all over the world.

Dr. Seligman is a bestselling author. His accomplishments include 15 books and 150 articles on motivation. His most sought-after books are Learned Optimism (Knopf, 1991), What You Can Change & What You Can't (Knopf, 1993), The Optimistic Child (Houghton Mifflin, 1995), Helplessness (Freeman, 1975, 1993) and Abnormal Psychology (Norton, 1982, 1988, 1995, with David Rosenhan).

Among other prominent awards he is the recipient of two Distinguished Scientific Contribution awards from the American Psychological Association, the Laurel Award of the American Association for Applied Psychology and Prevention, and the Lifetime Achievement Award of the Society for Research in Psychopathology.

TIPS

- Keep negative emotions and impulses under control.
- Take responsibility for negative behavior of your past and present actions.
- Recognize your strengths and weaknesses.
- Strive to improve on all your personal accomplishments.
- Recognize and understand the importance of optimism in job performance and success.
- Develop the practice of taking direct feedback and criticism of any negative actions.

 *Summary*

1. Practice emotional intelligence in all aspects of your life.
2. Learn to recognize and deal with circumstances that cause stress.
3. Practice empathy and keep an open mind to improve all your shortcomings.
4. Train your mind to feel the impact of your emotions on the sensations and reflexes of your body.
5. Develop a strong Emotional Quotient to live by your principles, morals and the sense of right behavior.

Chapter 9

Body Language Techniques to Succeed

SECTION I

"When the eyes say one thing, and the tongue another, a practiced man relies on the language of the first."

–RALPH WALDO EMERSON

Thought – Emotion – Gesture

Body language - referred to as kinesics communication - is the interpretation and understanding of non-verbal communication based on scientific facts. CharlesDarwin in the late 1800s is regarded as the earliest expert to have made serious scientific observation regarding non-verbal communication. This understanding helps employers determine the potential, attitude and the ability of a person to work. Body language can have a strong impact on the outcome of an interview.

It is commonly believed that 93% of emotions, disappointment and anger are conveyed through body language. Sending and receiving signs takes place on both the conscious and unconscious level. Gestures often occur in clusters of signals and postures. The correct interpretation of thoughts, feelings and gestures in another person requires skill, patience and close observation. According to research 7% of a conversation is done through speech, 38% by the tone of voice, and 55% through body language. Nearly 90% of the opinion about others is formed in the first 4 minutes and 60 to 80% of it is through body language. The use of positive gestures improves speech, clears thought and helps overcome anxiety.

Eye Signals

Eyes reveal a lot of emotions and thoughts. We can interpret and understand the feeling of happiness, sadness, fear, love, surprise, honesty, jealousy and fatigue from the eyes a lot more than we believe. Positive feelings unconsciously cause the eyes to open wider while negative thoughts cause the pupils to contract.

Neuro-Linguistic Programming describes how we make observations through our sensory representational system based on visual, sound, feelings and logical thinking.

Eyes Looking Top Right

Recalling recent experiences and logical thinking.

Eyes Looking Top Left

Thinking about past experiences and emotions.

Eyes Looking Right

Creating a sound.

Eyes Looking Left

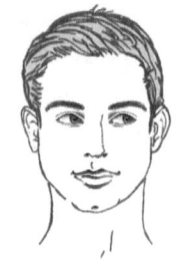

Recalling a sound.

Eyes Looking-Up

A sign of deep thinking, involving both logic and emotions.

Eyes Looking - Left
Indicates deep thought with oneself.

Eyes Looking Down - Right
Indicates a person who is questioning their feelings about something

Eyes Looking - Down
Submission, a feeling of guilt, also conveys a feeling of disinterest.

Direct Eye Contact

Direct eye contact during an interview is a crucial indication of trust and honesty. A direct eye contact conveys the level of confidence, interest and professionalism of a job candidate. According to body language experts, not making direct contact is interpreted as dishonesty, deceit and fabrication of facts. In the western world including the United States of America, UK, Australia and Western Europe, direct eye contact conveys good manners. This habit makes the candidates appear more likeable and appealing during an interview.

Research has shown that too strong an eye contact can convey lies. After a prolonged stare, some liars all of a sudden look away and then look again. This is an unconscious gesture to see if the listener has caught on to their deceit.

On the other hand, in countries like China and Japan, direct eye contact is considered inappropriate. It is considered a sign of disrespect. In African and Latin American countries direct eye contact is considered aggressive and extremely disrespectful.

Before an interview, negotiation or interaction, it is advisable to study the appropriate body language of different cultures.

Smile

Even though, a smile is universally accepted to express true feelings, happiness and acceptance, it can convey separate feeling and emotions based on the individual person's thinking, circumstances and behavior.

■ The Empowered Employee

Tight-Lipped Smile

This smile is used as a secret gesture, to hide a feeling, often adopted by women to conceal emotions.

Drop - Jaw Smile

Adopted by artists to draw the immediate attention of the viewers, often used by public figures, during speeches and press conferences.

Fake Smile

The eyes remain open, - (big wide eyes). No wrinkles on the side of both the eyes, visible bottom teeth.

Genuine Smile

A sincere effort, it conveys a feeling of trust and sincerity. The cheeks enlarge. Wrinkles form on the outer edge of the eyes. Both the eyes close when the cheeks move upwards.

Turn Away Smile

This smile conveys mischief, and playfulness, used to attract instant attention.

SECTION II

Open Palm Gesture needs to be hidden.

A palm fully opened indicates openness, conveying a completely non-threatening attitude.

- Palm(s)-finger's point up indicates - Authority
- Palm(s)-down indicates - Strength
- Palm moving up and down as if weighing indicates - Seeking answers
- Hand(s) on heart (left side of chest) indicates - Seeking to be believed
- Finger pointing (at a person) indicates - Threat
- Finger point and wink indicates - Acknowledgement
- Finger pointing (in the air) indicates - Emphasis
- Clenched fist(s) indicates - Determination
- Cracking knuckles indicates – Attention-seeking
- Interwoven clenched fingers indicates - Frustration

Important Body Language Gestures

Straight Head

This is a sign of a person with a neutral attitude. The head usually remains still and the neck balances directly over the spine. The hand to cheek gesture is often used with this position.

Tilted Head

A sign of submission, exposing the neck and throat, makes a person appear less threatening. Women are more likely to use this position than men.

Stalling

A tactic used to delay a verdict at the time of making a decision. Folding the glasses conveys an intention to end the discussion. Throwing the glasses on the table, symbolizes the desire to reject the proposal.

Ear Rub

A signal that the person has heard enough, an attempt by the listener to block words being heard and is ready to respond.

Neck Scratch

The index finger of the right hand scratches below the ear, an unconscious gesture of doubt and uncertainty when the mind does not agree with the words spoken.

Nose Touch

Touching the part of the face below the nose and above the mouth conveys lying. This is often seen when someone is not speaking the entire truth or when someone is suspicious of another person lying. In addition, it signifies anxiety and nervousness.

■ The Empowered Employee

Eye Rub

A common practice, rubbing the eye is an indication of being tired, used more often by children. In adults it conveys doubt or lying. In some instances, it can be used as a gesture during a conversation, to avoid sharing of thoughts. This gesture is used more by men than women.

Open Legs

This gesture is a sign of an open and dominant attitude which can offend others. Sitting with legs wide apart before a woman can be interpreted as sexual interest.

Steeple

A sign of confidence, most often adopted by a person in power. Also, used to convey a self-assured approach towards a particular task.

Crossed Arm

The crossed-arm sign conveys a feeling of insecurity, nervousness and a negative attitude. It can also be used by someone in deep thought and can happen due to a sudden drop in temperature.

One Crossed Arm

A partial barrier of a single arm across the chest signifies the need for protection, adopted as a cover to shield from unknown surroundings or unfamiliar people.

Power Gaze

A triangle is formed between the eyes and the forehead. A steady gaze lasting no more than two seconds is used to influence or convey a firm decision.

Social Gaze

A triangle forms between the eyes and the nose or the mouth. This is one of the easiest and friendly gazes. It helps build rapport and conveys a friendly and unbiased approach.

Hands Clasped Behind Head

This gesture is most often used by men in authority, conveys a sense of superiority and confidence. A sign of not feeling threatened and being at ease. Job candidates may see this gesture used by an interviewer who is in a senior position.

Shoulder Shrug

A gesture of raised shoulders conveys not knowing about something or someone, accompanied by raised eyebrows and open palms, conveys submission, uncertainty or a lack of understanding.

Critical Thinking

The index finger points towards the cheek and covers the mouth. The thumb supports the chin. A sign of critical and skeptical thinking.

SECTION III

Chin Stroking

A sign of deep contemplation during a decision-making process. Most often used by men.

Hands in the Pocket

This is a sign of dominance, superiority or aggression. Both thumbs sticking out of the pocket of a male is a sign of attracting female attention.

Legs Crossed

Standing with arms folded and legs crossed indicates fear and a lack of confidence. In a man it conveys the need to protect his masculinity, in a woman it can be interpreted as someone who is distant and not easily approachable.

Hands in Raised Position

This gesture conveys a negative thought. During a negotiation it means the person is holding back or is anxious about getting the cooperation of others. Adopted from the Italians and French, it can reveal frustration, even while smiling.

Hands Clenched in Middle Position

A seemingly relaxed gesture actually means the person is going through the feeling of frustration and anxiety, feeling the need to restrain negative actions.

Broken - Zipper Posture

Hands placed low and in front of the waist is a sign of a man protecting his masculinity. This gesture is often used in public places to overcome the feeling of vulnerability.

Legs Crossed

This gesture typically conveys a female's sense of modesty and the desire to keep a correct posture. Legs held tightly together are also a sign of anxiety and self-restraint.

The Mirroring Gesture

Mirroring is a natural response to imitate another person's expressions and gestures. Activated by a special class of brain cells, this leads to similarity of emotions between two people. It consciously promotes the feeling of security and cooperation.

Open Triangle Posture

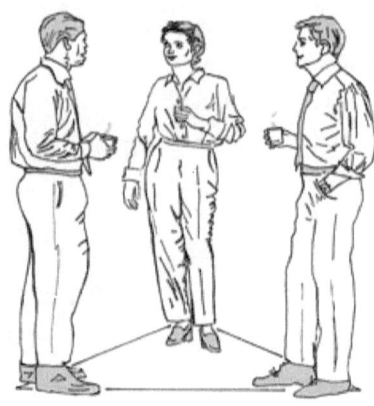

The distance of 45-degress between the first two people encourages the entry of the third person in the discussion. This builds rapport and camaraderie in the workplace, networking forums and community events.

Behind Back Position

Behind Back Hand Grip

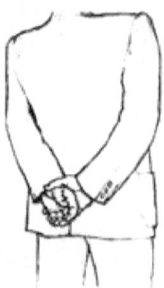

An indication of superiority and confidence. This posture is mostly adopted by leaders, and those in a position of power.

Behind Back Wrist Grip

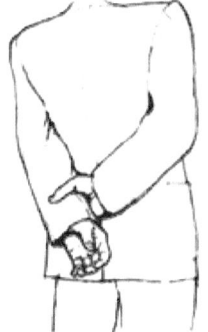

This is a sign of holding back, an attempt to control the hand from reacting to a situation, conveys a feeling of frustration.

Behind Back Elbow Grip

Similar to the Wrist Grip, this gesture conveys a greater need for self-control in a negative situation.

Cross-Cultural Rule of Thumb

A sign almost universally, accepted as Good, OK, or Hitchhike. Indicates the number 'one' in Germany. Conveys an uncomplimentary gesture in Australia, Nigeria.

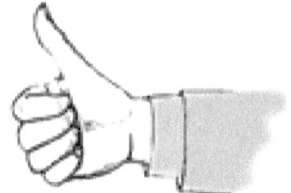

■ The Empowered Employee

A common hand gesture, mostly interpreted as sign of disproval or refusal. In France, Germany and Hungary, this can be interpreted as the number "one".

This would be interpreted by an American as "two". Signifies "victory" to a German. On the other hand it is taken as a sign of insult in Britain.

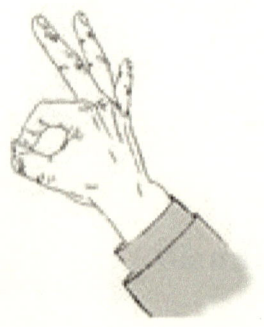

A sign of "OK" to a British and American national. A sexual insult to a Russian, and those belonging to the Mediterranean regions. A signal of being "worthless" in France. Conveys "money" in Japan.

The V is considered a gesture of peace in the United States and Japan. It indicates offense in United Kingdom, South Africa, Australia, New Zealand and Ireland. A sign of being cute during a photo shoot in China, Japan, South Korea, Taiwan and Thailand.

Master the Art of Handshaking

A handshake reveals a great deal about a person. Invariably everyone has received a bad handshake. A perfect handshake conveys sincerity.

- A common and popular greeting during a handshake is – "nice to meet you".
- Wrap your thumb and fingers all the way around your partner's hand. Shake 3 to 4 times and press assertively.
- A formal handshake should last between 3 to 6 seconds.
- The distance between two people in a business environment should be 2ft to 4ft from each other.
- Never put your left hand in a trouser pocket during a hand shake.
- Make no comment about a handshake, even if it does not feel right.
- An improper handshake leaves a negative feeling. You will be closely assessed by the way you shake hands with a stranger.
- Maintain an open and positive posture during a handshake, smile, make eye contact, and introduce yourself with your first and last name.
- During the first meeting, address the person by name. Use the salutation of (Mr., Ms., Mrs., and Dr.) and their last name. This rule is applicable for both men and women.
- Do not shake hands directly across a desk during an interview.
- A handshake with your palms down will put you at an immediate disadvantage.
- A good handshake needs constant practice, confidence and sincerity.
- When meeting people from other countries, you need to research cultural differences. Make sure not to offend their cultural sensitivity with an inappropriate handshake.

An equal handshake conveys a feeling of mutual respect. Both the palms face each other, and remain in a vertical position. Sometimes you may have to adjust the position, to balance the pressure between the hands.

Handshake Equality

The double-grip handshake conveys a sign of superiority and power. It can convey a negative impression in a formal meeting. Do not feel obligated to return a double handshake.

Handshake Double Grip

The palm faces down to grasp the hand of the other person. This gesture conveys the feeling of wanting to have the "upper hand" in a situation. A study revealed that nearly 90% of senior management executive initiate, this handshake.

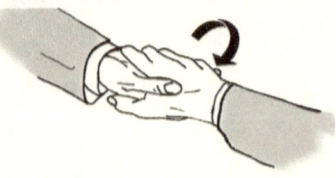
Handshake Taking Conrol

The Wrist Grip

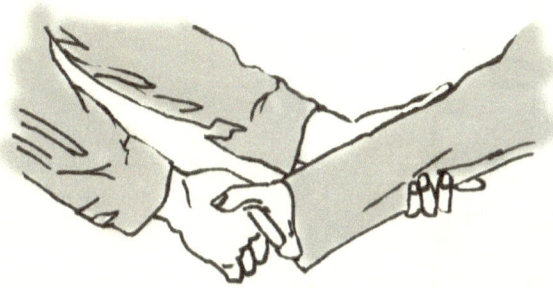

This gesture is adopted as a form of greeting where a personal and emotional bond exists between two people. It is a clear indication of intensifying the bond.

The Elbow Hold

This gesture should be initiated only where there is a mutual feeling of closeness. Otherwise it can be interpreted as intruding in the personal space of the other person.

Body Language Mistakes to Avoid

Finger Pointing

A gesture of authority, interpreted as angry and violent. This show of arrogance is considered impolite and inappropriate in a business and social environment.

Staring

The intensity of the stare reveals a lot about a person's thoughts and reaction. Prolonged eye contact can make the on-looker feel uncomfortable and threatened.

Distance between People

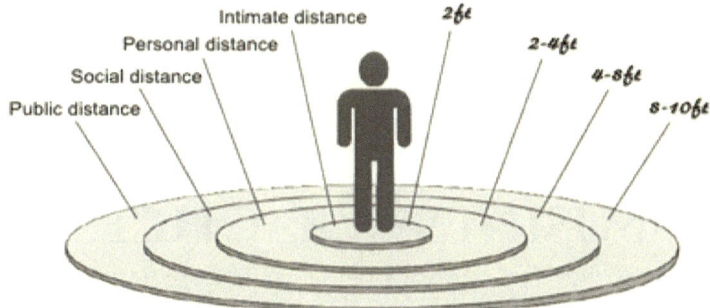

 TIPS

- Learn and practice body language skills.
- Closely observe the body language of others.
- Attempt to always leave a positive and lasting impression.
- Read signs in direct context to the situation and circumstances.
- Direct eye contact most often conveys truth and honesty, in some cultures it can be misinterpreted as being aggressive.
- Control the urge to use aggressive signs and gestures.
- Touching jewelry and other accessories conveys insecurity and anxiety.

 *Summary*

1. Learn to effectively use the power of body language.
2. Rehearse sitting and standing postures.
3. Practice the various forms of handshakes.
4. Study the social and business etiquettes of different cultures.
5. Learn to identify different body language postures and gestures.

Chapter 10

Ethical Principles In Business Practices

"Apart from values and ethics which I have tried to live by, the legacy I would like to leave behind is a very simple one - that I have always stood up for what I consider to be the right thing, and I have tried to be as fair and equitable as I could be"

–RATAN TATA

Business ethics, also known as Corporate Ethics, reflects the importance of integrity, and trust in individual behavior and company practices. Careful planning should be adopted in shaping the ethics policy of an organization. The policy should be implemented in every decision-making process and practiced in the day-to-day operations on both the organizational and functional levels.

To maintain the highest standards of ethics, all employees must be treated with equal fairness and respect. Employers need to promote equal opportunity and diversity. No employee should be discriminated against on the basis of age, gender, religion, caste, and marital status or mental or physical disability. To avoid and curb such instances, every employee should be made liable to report any form of unlawful activity against them or other employees.

Leading multinational companies implement the best corporate ethics policy to ensure their core values and decision-making process is beyond conflict and personal interest. The objective is to develop a strong sense of values in every employee to act ethically and legally. The policies are usually amended from time to time, to keep up with the legal requirements and regulations.

Core Values

Four Ways to Develop Workplace Ethics

Integrity

A primary source of integrity and trustworthiness is shaped by culture, a form of behavior every employee is expected to follow. Actions are evaluated based on four common standards of etiquettes, integrity, morality and trust. Reliability directly impacts output. An effective ethical policy of an organization compels each employee to achieve greater success by being honest, truthful and reliable. All employees are obligated to keep company information private. In the words of English writer, humorists and dramatist, Douglas Adams, *"To give real service you must add something which cannot be bought or measured with money, and that is sincerity and integrity."*

Loyalty

Employees are passionate and committed to providing the highest quality of service. Even though the term organizational loyalty has undergone a major change, implementing a "reward system" will inculcate trust and increase commitment. Encourage employees, to align their goals with the company's objective. This will increase productivity and improve the work dynamics. According to former American basketball player, Scott Brooks, "The best kind of loyalty is when both parties are benefiting."

Responsibility

Responsible employees control behavior through a strong moral code of ethics. They follow ethical principles, set new standards for other employees and obey laws. The ethics policy of a company should clearly outline, that employees must be made accountable for any unfair practices towards other employees, customers and clients.

■ The Empowered Employee

Output

Increased employee output is most critical for a business to succeed. This can only be achieved through satisfied, loyal and productive employees. Most senior executives have assessed that their workforce is operating at only 60% to 65% of their full potential. According to a recent survey conducted by a leading HR consultancy firm, employee output was recorded at 59% only. This is a reality no organization can ignore. "Managers can maximize output by 30%. They should adopt a proactive approach, examine their own management style, motivate and coach each employee to achieve higher levels of performance."

Tips

- Maintain high standards of honesty and integrity.
- Align work with personal values and goals.
- Make morally correct, informed and intelligent decisions.

Summary

1. Understand the need to implement a culture of strong ethics in an organization.
2. Study the ethics policy of your company, to build a healthy relationship between individual and organizational values and beliefs.
3. Practice strong individual values, in families, communities and social organizations.
4. Develop qualities to be a role model to create a more ethical work environment.
5. Learn to take decision based on what is right and individually correct in every given situation.

Chapter 11

Career Action Plan

"Great works are performed not by strength, but by perseverance."
– SAMUEL JOHNSON

Career planning is about finding your mission in life with a vision of the future. Before setting a goal, the question to keep in mind is, why am I doing this and how is it going to impact my future? Do not succumb to blind ambition by setting unapproachable goals. Set clear and written goals and a plan to accomplish them by setting a firm deadline.

Planning

A carefully planned strategy can be executed with the desired result in mind. A successful outcome depends on your ability to follow your plan with energy, focus, passion, and the desire to win against all odds. Finding your mission in life, and understanding your goals and desires clearly will help define a successful career path.

Purpose

A keen sense of purpose and a heartfelt commitment gives rise to the feeling of enthusiasm. It gets you the cooperation of other people, and a sense of motivation. It is a powerful force which helps you carry out the thoughts, you constantly hold in your mind with a desirable purpose. In the words of Gautama Buddha, "Your purpose in life is to find your purpose and give your whole heart and soul to it."

Vision

Visualize the kind of job you want. It should be specific in terms of your needs, desires, goals and objectives. The method of using imagination to develop a perfect image of achieving your goals and objectives has been proven to attract the desired results. Think and bring circumstances into your life.

Passion

People, who are able to bring passion to their work, have a remarkable advantage to succeed in comparison to those who lack initiative, and the willingness to take risks.

According to famous American writer Dale Carnegie, "Most of the important things in the world have been accomplished by people who kept on trying when there seemed to be no hope at all."

Rationale

To succeed, recognize a realistic expectation of your goals. Although, no goal is impossible to achieve, setting a standard would help you better evaluate the time, hard work, and commitment required to accomplish your objective.

Once two friends, Steve and Ryan, were discussing their future plans. Steve said, "I want to earn a five-figure salary in the next five years." Ryan's ambition was to become the Chief Executive Officer of a large organization. Since, Steve had set a broader goal for himself, he was able to accomplish his purpose faster than Ryan.

Persistence

Intelligent persistence is that "MAGIC" word that helps overcome the feelings of doubt, fear and criticism. Positive thinkers use it as an inspiration to develop faith and courage in pursuing their desired goals.

Self-Discipline

Self-discipline is creating and following specific rules to accomplish all goals and objectives. Developing discipline requires a lot of courage, and focus. This holds true at all times, and for all people of all age groups. It is easy to stay focused when things are easy, the challenge is when things get tough, and aren't going your way. A strong sense of discipline will help you stay focused, measure your success, and if the need arises, develop new plans.

In the words of famous English biologist Thomas Henry Huxley, "Perhaps the most valuable result of all education is the ability to make yourself do the thing you have to do, whether you like it or not."

Self-Belief

Self-belief is to develop a firm faith in your abilities. The aim should be, to overcome all fears, and experience the feeling of being a "winner". Research has proved that persons with an Internal Locus of Control are in complete control of their lives, and very much in charge of their destiny. Recognize your true self-worth, and value your education, skills and accomplishments, at the same time, accept your weaknesses, and work towards overcoming them.

Professionalism

The Merriam-Webster dictionary defines professionalism as "the conduct, aims, or qualities that characterize or mark a profession or a professional person". A professional, is recognized by a deep sense of commitment to do their best in every situation. They never compromise their value and maintain a strict moral conduct in all situations, by taking complete responsibility for all their thoughts, words, and actions. True professionals are the first to be considered for promotions, and they are awarded valuable projects or clients, which make them routinely successful in their careers. *According to British-born American journalist Alistair Cooke, "A professional is someone who can do his best work when he doesn't feel like it."*

Flexibility

A flexible strategy will help redirect, and modify your plan according to the change in circumstances. A variable approach will further help you overcome the fear of failure, and rejection. Choosing one career path, in the early years of employment, need not necessarily eliminate other options. It is important to find the right balance by taking short-term opportunities, and gradually build them into long-term career goals.

Opportunity

The ability to identify and evaluate the right opportunity is rarely accepted as a skill for students and jobseekers. To recognize opportunities similar to your interest, to act on it and succeed is a challenge in itself. You need to be focused and current in identifying every available opportunity. Regular online research and networking are two of the most effective and powerful ways to find employment. A new set of opportunities will open up if you create an online profile and sign up for Google alerts.

■ The Empowered Employee

Attend trade shows and conventions. Contact employers directly. Email or call them to introduce yourself, keep the right attitude, tell the truth and never give up.

Alternate Career Plan

Set an alternate career option in advance. This will need time, energy, expertise and planning. American author Helen Keeler who led a courageous and highly inspiring life said, "Change: A bend in the road is not the end of the road... Unless you fail to make the turn."

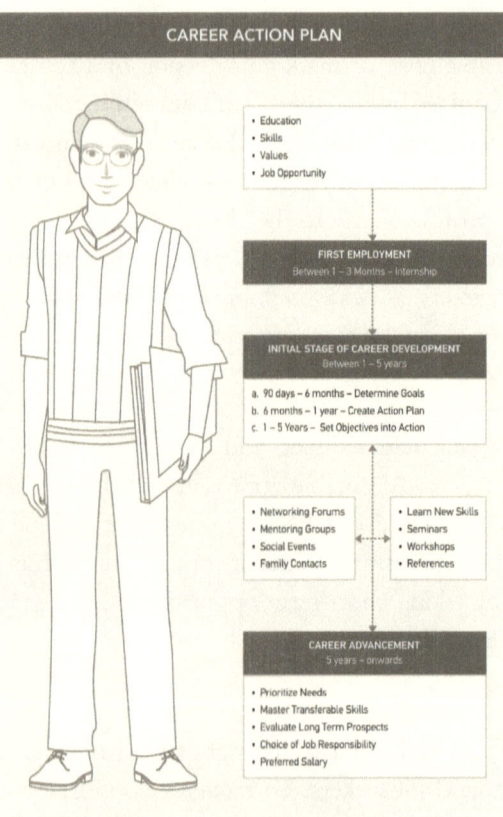

TIPS

- Do not be intimated or envy the success of your peers.
- Start by setting professional and financial goals.
- Set a deadline to accomplish your goals.
- Organize your goals by sequence and priority.
- Do something every day to achieve your goals.

Summary

1. In order of preference, write down all the goals you wish to accomplish.
2. Set a time frame to accomplish each goal.
3. Task I = No. of weeks to complete.
4. Task II = No. of months to complete.
5. Task III = No. of Years to complete.
6. Evaluate all your achievements at the end of each week.
7. Develop an achievable career strategy to accomplish your goals.
8. Set alternate career goals.

Chapter 12

Develop Advanced Communication Skills

"Communication works for those who work at it."

– JOHN POWELL

Five Steps to Effective Verbal Communication

Conversation

The essential skill of today's professional, is to have the ability to communicate with clarity, persuasion and confidence. The art of effective conversation needs practice. An outstanding conversationalist is a pleasure to converse with. Words and the tone of voice, expressed by such individuals are effortless, and fluent. Constantly remaining alert, and monitoring what you reveal is important. A skilled conversationalist keeps complete control over their thoughts, and emotions.

Disagreements and disputes destroy the true spirit of a good conversation. A talk succeeds best when everyone in the group participates with the same interest and enthusiasm. Sensitive topics like intimate personal details, religion, and politics, should be strictly avoided in a professional conversation.

Listening

Listening involves patience, and the desire to understand what the other person is saying. In some instances, saying less than necessary is essential. Avoid the risk of communicating anything that is inappropriate or offensive.

Speech

An effective speaking skill needs energy, creativity, ideas, and vision. Perfecting facial expressions and overcoming the feeling of fear and insecurity are the three most powerful tools for conquering communication barriers. A good conversationalist practices patience, and the skill to understand the other person. No matter what the response, by no means react with disappointment to a negative comment or statement. Join Toastmasters International, or similar 'Meet-Up' groups to learn or improve public speaking and presentation skills.

Attention

A good conversationalist has the ability to draw the attention of their listener without using forceful words or by trying to use undue influence. Best described in the words of Jim Rohn, "Take advantage of every opportunity to practice your communication skills, so that when important occasions arise, you will have the gift, the style, the sharpness, the clarity and the emotions to effect other people."

Emotion

Emotions cannot be ignored. People react only when their feelings are aroused. A perfect conversationalist recognizes the impact of positive emotions in day-to-day conversation. Sensitivity and kindness are the hallmark of success. A person without feelings cannot have a sincere and frank conversation. This sense reinforces courtesy, manners and etiquette in persons. Regardless of the situation, individuals make a conscious effort to understand and cooperate with each other.

Sarcasm

Be particularly careful not to use sarcasms. No matter how compelling a sarcastic comment feels, avoid an impolite response. Disrespect and mockery will overshadow the most cordial and pleasant conversation.

Chain of Thought

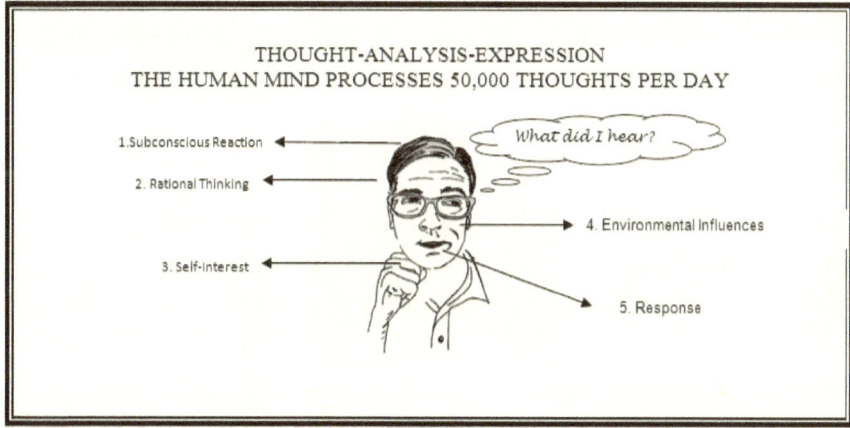

Develop Business Writing Skills

Business writing is the ability to write intelligently, and compose powerful and professional documents. To sound effective, persons often tend to use complex words. You express yourself more clearly, if you use short sentences, and simple language. Before starting to write, have the end in mind. This will help you develop an effective flow of thought and description.

Good business writing is an impressive tool that supports and values your skill, education, and work experience. Employers generally believe that only 30% of college and university graduates have the ability to write correct business language. Writing skills can make a big difference to your efficiency, productivity, and career success. Just because someone is not a writer by profession, does not mean the ability to write cannot be developed in them. The desire to write, and the initiative to improve on grammar, and vocabulary can make anyone a good writer.

Rules of Business Writing

Practice

Good business writing needs practice. Frequently update your writing style, to fit the changing standards in the business environment. Avoid old-fashioned phrases, overused words and jargon. The more you write, the more you learn. In the words of Epictetus, Greek sage and Stoic philosopher, "If you wish to be a writer, write."

Purpose

Start by stating your purpose quickly. The aim should be to instantly hold the attention of the reader. This clearly communicates that you have something valuable to say. A well-written letter is persuasive, effective, and sensitive to the reader.

Reader

Organize your thoughts keeping the reader in mind. Business writing is inextricably tied to company identity: writers have to think about, what a company stands for, its goals, objectives, and how the company should be represented in public.

Sentence

Business letters follow a specific format. Write short sentences to convey important information in a professional way. Use active instead of passive verbs. Active verbs help to energize your purpose. Instead of writing "The meeting was led by Tom", write: "Tom led the meeting". Use easy-to-read sentences: Subject + Verb + Object. Be cautious about subject-verb confusion and grammar.

Effect and Affect

The similarities between these words cause much confusion in writing.

"Effect "is a noun meaning outcome, consequences or appearance.

"Affect" is a verb, meaning to transform or change.

Layout

The layout of a business letter is as important as what you write. A poorly formatted letter will turn away the interest of the reader.

Margin

Business letter margins should be about 1" all around. The text should align to the left. This will make the letter more readable, striking, and give it an uncluttered look.

Spacing

The letter should be aligned to the left and single-spaced. No double space in between sentences, except for a double space in-between the paragraphs. Use one space after a period or full stop.

Font Style

There is no need to use different font styles in a professional letter. Use a uniform font *(a book-print font such as Times New Roman or Arial)*. Avoid underlining words and limit the use of bold letters.

Font

Arial and Times New Roman are the standard fonts used in business letters. Use a font size between 10 and 12 points.

Language

Plain language ensures that readers can easily understand. Omit the use of words like "quite," "mostly," "slightly," "seems," "sort of," "pretty," and "somewhat".

Draft

To get good results, make a note of all the main points in the form of a draft. Create attention-getting subject lines. Salutations, openings, and closing sentences are the most important parts of writing.

Clarity

Clarity in thought and expressions are two of the most important aspects for effective business writing. To express the main points precisely, requires skill, and constant practice. In the initial stages of your writing, seek feedback from a skilled writer.

Proofread

Identify and recognize unnecessary words, phrases and repetition. Correct grammatical mistakes, choice of words or spelling errors. Also, double-check statistics or other figures mentioned. Always use the black and white format only, black letters on white paper.

Legal Requirement

A simple error in business communication can lead to severe legal consequences. Do not violate rules and regulations. When in doubt, consult a legal professional for advice.

- Communicate with confidence and use persuasive language.
- Limit the use of verbs in business writing.
- Do not use metaphors, similes or any slang words.
- Do not confuse between "affect" and "effect".
- Avoid the use of exclamation marks.

Summary

1. Practice the art of formal and informal conversation.
2. Practice business writing skills by composing formal letters and memos.
3. Learn commonly used business abbreviations and idioms.
4. Use specific business terms while speaking to peers, and clients, and during presentations.
5. Develop the skills to hold a conversation in a clear and polite manner.
6. Participate in forums like Toastmasters International to improve your conversation and presentation skills.

Chapter 13

Guidelines for a Group Discussion

"Discussion is the exchange of knowledge; argument is the exchange of ignorance."
– ROBERT QUILLEN

Fundamental Rules of a Group Discussion

A group discussion is a popular method adopted by a large number of companies, to evaluate the level of competence, general knowledge, attitude, self-confidence and communication in candidates. It's a process where your ideas and opinions are debated upon.

Topics

General topics in a group discussion during an interview include leadership, information and technology, health, environment, unemployment, child labour, inflation, sports, social media and youth in politics.

Through a group discussion, employers judge a candidate's ability to be open-minded, explore alternative views, generate multiple options, and handle high-pressure situations. The participants have to monitor their thinking, remain alert, and display the ability to exercise control over their thoughts and feelings.

The important topics discussed are on politics, current issues, sports, and general knowledge. The discussion is usually between 20-30 minutes in length. A group of three to five participants are seated in a roundtable.

Rules

A well-structured group discussion follows a specific set of rules. It starts with a formal introduction. Each participant gives an introduction of themselves, including name and a brief profile. Before the beginning of the discussion a few minutes is given to the members to interact with, and build rapport among each other.

Manners

The participants must respect the personal space of each other. Always lift your right hand to take permission to speak. Personal items should not be placed on the table. The discussion should not be interrupted by the ringing of a cell phone, a whisper or any other inappropriate or loud gestures.

Participation

There should be equal participation from all candidates; each participant is expected to build the conversation with a personal viewpoint, add new ideas, and develop the discussion. The responses should be short, and directed towards a particular goal. Respect the views of others, and make sure not to always try and appear "right".

Pronunciation

To be an effective communicator, it is important to have excellent command over language. Right accent, choice of words, correct tone of voice, pauses, and repetitions are closely observed by the interviewer. The right style of speaking is also an important indicator of a person's education, background, mannerism, and values.

Confidence

A self-assured attitude helps develop confidence, overcome nervousness, fear, and shyness. A strong sense of self-belief makes it easier to rise above inhibitions, and self-imposed restrictions.

Perception

It is best to adopt a practical viewpoint. A rational approach is automatically accepted. A potential employee, who demonstrates the ability to handle a situation, in a practical manner, is appreciated. A candidate must display, good cognitive abilities, the willingness to explore, to inquire, take intellectual risks, and the ability to think critically and imaginatively. In-depth thinking helps candidates to further stretch their knowledge and imagination.

Tact

Contradictions or counter arguments should be strictly avoided. Disagreements should be brushed aside gently, and with tact. No candidate should try, and challenge the intellectual ability of other participants. Any form of disagreement, should be handled in a polite manner. Justify a difference in opinion preferably with examples and facts.

Tolerance

It is very important for each participant to remain tolerant. No form of disrespect or inappropriate language will be allowed by the moderator. If the discussion turns argumentative or aggressive, the moderator has the right to immediately disqualify the participant from the group.

Cooperation

A collective approach demonstrates the ability of a candidate to work in teams, and recognize opportunities for collaboration.

Persuasion

The ability to persuade a group is an important indicator of managerial success, and problem-solving skills in a candidate.

Listening

Active listening and concentration is required to succeed in a group discussion. A well-developed ability to pay attention will give a candidate greater advantage over the other participants.

Criticism

The ability to take criticism displays a candidate's capacity to handle emotions, and control impulses. The courage to admit to your mistakes, and accept weaknesses is highly appreciated by employers.

Recalling

Recall is the test of memory, and reflective skills. It highlights productive behavior in terms of recalling names and the key points discussed.

Closing

Summarize the important points discussed by the participants. Evaluate the arguments and facts. Avoid raising new viewpoints at the end. Present your observation, then clearly define and explain with examples on how you reached this conclusion. A balanced viewpoint will make you appear neutral and unbiased. Unless there is a real reason, never interrupt or speak while another participant is closing the discussion. Plan and take the initiative to conclude the discussion. This will give you the chance to earn extra points at the end.

Eye Contact

During the course of a discussion, it is important to maintain direct eye contact with the other participants. Observing eye signals help the employer judge the honesty, straightforwardness and level of confidence in a candidate.

Body Movement and Gestures

- ➢ Sitting with the right posture reflects refined manners and etiquettes.
- ➢ Confidence is the key to success in a group discussion.
- ➢ Hand movements should be controlled and carefully monitored.
- ➢ Do not wrap your arms around your chest or cross your legs.
- ➢ Proper coordination between words and gestures displays control and restraint.

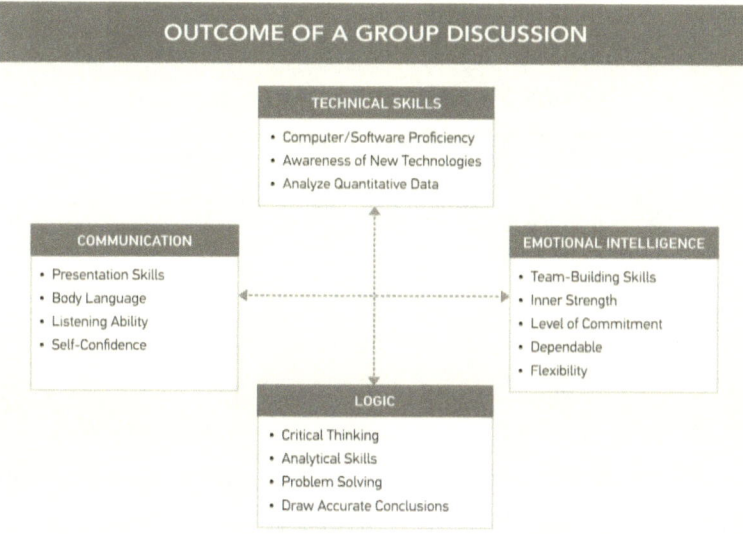

TIPS

- Gather sufficient information on popular and current topics.
- Organize your thoughts objectively.
- During the debate do not interrupt without seeking permission.
- Practice your tone of voice, speech and gestures effectively.

Summary

1. Stay well informed on current topics in politics, business, sports, entertainment and major events.
2. Learn the skill of persuasion and tact.
3. Practise group discussion with a minimum of three to four participants.
4. Learn to participate actively and put forward valuable points during a group discussion.
5. Increase your speaking ability.

Chapter 14

Develop a Corporate Image

"You make a first impression and people will never forget it."

– DIABLO CODY

Self-image has a great impact on the career of every professional. Nearly all employers closely observe appearance, formal style of dressing, mannerisms, posture and behavior of a candidate during an interview. Personality is of greater importance where employees have to represent the culture of their company through face-to-face interaction with customers e.g. sales, public relations and media, to name a few.

It is common to interpret a clean and tidy look with individuals who take care of themselves. A large number of experimental studies have shown significant correlation between appearance, competence and motivation. Good looks are often associated with higher level of intelligence, values and beliefs. Attractive persons are considered warmer, stronger, honest, interesting, and makers of their own destiny.

Formal dressing is associated with high-status jobs. It conveys a feeling of power and status, and helps in cultural integration between diverse groups of employees. Persons from different cultures can relate better when they dress in a similar fashion.

Essential Qualities for a Lasting Impression

Outer Image

In the very beginning of your career, it is important to develop a distinct personal **'Style'** with qualities and behavior that sets you apart and complements your skills and accomplishments in the corporate environment. A good posture, direct eye contact, positive attitude, and polite manners will make you stand out in terms of intellect, style and culture.

Inner Strength

A compassionate and generous approach is the hallmark of a born leader. Learn to smile from within. Self-awareness not only inspires confidence, but also invites others to have the desire to know you better.

Self-Esteem

Self-esteem can be developed with a strong sense of self-worth, a passion to succeed. The willingness to change and overcome shortcomings makes it easier to increase self-esteem, and overcome anxiety and insecurity.

Confidence

A self-assured attitude and positive body language conveys competence. It draws us out of our inhibitions and self-imposed restrictions. According to Peter T McIntyre, painter and author, "Confidence comes from not always being right but from not fearing to be wrong."

Creativity

Choosing the right dress style requires a great deal of practice and imagination. Creativity enhances the skills of dressing well. People who most often appeal to people's minds are artists, intellectuals, and those with a creative temperament. In the beginning of your career, it is good to consult an image management expert.

- Develop a fine sense of dress style. Seek professional help to enhance your style.
- Develop and practice self-confidence techniques.
- Remain observant of the fashion sense of your seniors and colleagues.
- Overcome interpersonal conflicts, and always compliment other people on their successes and accomplishments.

Summary

1. Take the time to enhance your personal appearance, so that your image can help your goals.
2. Identify the style of formal outfits and colours that suit your personality.
3. Always wear well-fitted clothes and shoes.
4. Purchase clothes only after a trial at the store. Seek the opinion of the sales staff about the texture of the outfit, suitable to formal dressing.
5. In the beginning of your career, seek the advice and guidance of an image management consultant.

Chapter 15

Cultivate Practical Management Wisdom

"We are made wise not by the recollection of our past, but by the responsibility of our future."

– GEORGE BERNARD SHAW

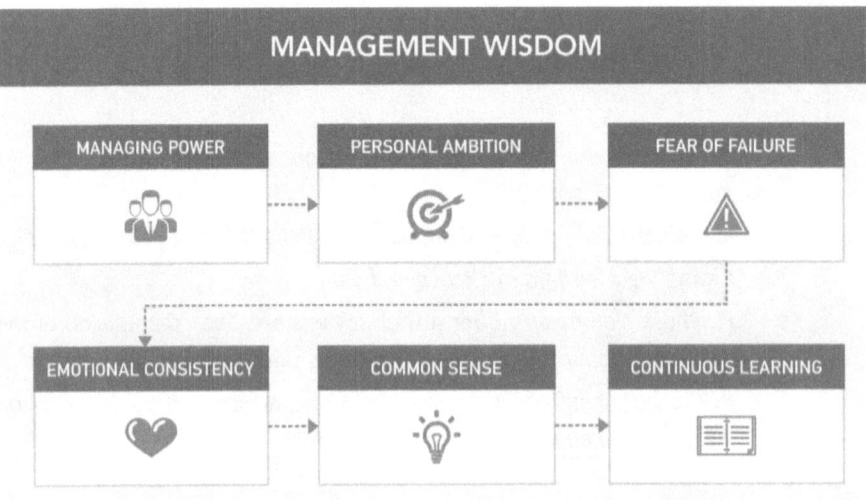

Managing Power

There are mainly two types of power to influence people and their behavior. One is external power derived from a person's official position and the other, internal power drawn from an individual's charisma and personality. There is a sharp dividing line between the two forces. Power needs to be handled in a responsible way. Excessive use of power can create conflict in the most cohesive and agreeable team. Peers and subordinates recognize both forms of power.

Charismatic and outstanding leaders create a balance between the two to build trust and achieve long-term success.

Personal Ambition

The true meaning of a sense of purpose is to look beyond self interest and individual goals. Reinvent the meaning of personal ambition by combining personal goals with company objectives. Adopt a more flexible approach. A formal division between the two creates inefficiency. A lack of passion and gaps comes in the way of long-term success. All of this leads to unnecessary implications and ends up becoming a burden, the manager does not feel motivated enough to perform tasks and lead through change.

Fear of Failure

Leadership needs a more rational approach to encourage the workers and go beyond traditional management techniques. An intense fear of failure lacks vision. The worry of being demoted, concern about performance appraisals or a job loss stops a person from taking risks, making mistakes and forcing change. The feeling of defeat that comes with it causes excessive anxiety. Failure is a great teacher. Learn to accept rejections and face bad decisions. According to the famous actor, comedian and author Bill Cosby, "In order to succeed, your desire for success should be greater than your fear of failure."

Emotional Consistency

Emotional consistency is crucial. It helps a leader remain tolerant in the face of challenges, execute plans, go the extra mile, handle financial crisis and regulate the workforce by making their performance more effective and consistent. It also allows their staff members to articulate their thoughts and nurture beneficial and emotionally satisfying relationships.

They are both intellectually and emotionally stimulating. The most important aspect for an emotionally competent leader is to keep a balance in the tone of voice, use subtle gestures and make a positive impact on others. Crucial to success, such leaders are able to take the right decision at the right time by arousing the emotions, energy and passion of the team members to achieve excellence and the desired results.

Common Sense

The most fundamental problem in leadership is the lack of common sense. One of the most essential qualities for leadership growth is often taken for granted and is highly underrated. Simple reasoning rather than facts and figures can help overcome enormous hurdles and obstacles within organizations. A practical approach applied to skills and abilities leads to better output.

How some people have more common sense than others lies in the fact that people who have more opportunities to deal with problems and cope with challenge are better at figuring things out and analyzing situations. The centre of leadership growth, it helps build effective relationships, trust and respect. This most basic tool to succeed gets overpowered by the lack of objectivity, greed and bias.

Continuous Learning

Strong leaders take the initiative and make it a practice to pursue knowledge and commit to continuous learning. They identify new ways to learn and keep current with ongoing change. The best leaders develop important skills to manage day-to-day situations across various industries and apply new strategies in the competitive work environment. Set higher goals and take action on them.

- Develop a long-term strategy, measure and predict present actions and future impacts.
- Concentrate on developing one skill at a time. Focus on what is most needed to succeed.
- Build and enhance a sense of responsibility and improvement.
- Build positive working relationships.
- Be vigilant - every action, word and thought counts.

Summary

1. Move out of your comfort zone and embrace change.
2. Develop the ability to see the big picture, chart new ideas, and break new grounds.
3. Recall the leaders you admire and follow their example.
4. Learn to bring together a large number of views that help in applying practical management wisdom.
5. Practice keeping an open mind while taking decisions.

Chapter 16

Build Global Networking Skills

....

"Meet New People to Extend Your Professional Network."

"It's all about people, it's about networking and being nice to people and not burning bridges."

– MIKE DAVIDSON

Global networking is the most powerful source to find a job. New positions are frequently debated, created, and funded, even before a single job advertisement is placed. In simple words, it is about establishing rapport with someone who is a complete stranger. A well-planned strategy can lead to immense corporate success. Successful people make attempts to get to know a lot of people through various disciplines of work, communities and public forums.

Networking takes time to build. The most important fact is to, never convey a self-centered approach. Positive networking initiatives are based on respect, and mutually rewarding relationships. Learn to give before you take in terms of a kind favour, or a generous act, as both go a long way in building positive and long-term associations.

Networking is about creating the right balance of power, through gratefulness, trust, and reputation. Subtle reminders of your presence are important. Keep the connection alive by regular contact through networking events, email and social media.

A prime example of volunteering is when I took the initiative to volunteer. Due to my commitment and hard work and sincerity, I got elected as a Board of Director for the prominent North Eastern Centre of Community Society in Calgary, Alberta, a prestigious $1.20 million project.

Powerful Networking Tips

Initiative

Networking is all about initiative and resourcefulness. Join professional organizations and meet up groups with common interests. Attempt to attend at least one activity every month. After you have proven yourself, you may ask for references and contacts of people who might help you further develop your skills and abilities to achieve professional excellence.

According to an old proverb, "It's not what you know, it's who you know." Done in the right way, it will generate powerful contacts and referrals for new business opportunities, and better job prospects.

Mutual Respect

Networking based on mutual respect yields maximum rewards. A high level of regard for your contact, will keep your association with them lifelong. People who can give without expecting anything in return, are the most successful people in any given field.

Reputation

A credible reputation is essential for growing, a strong business network. It is impossible to develop a strong network without a high level of integrity, trust, and faith. In the words of Mahatma Gandhi, "When I despair, I remember that all through history the way of truth and love have always won. There have been tyrants and murderers, and for a time, they can seem invincible, but in the end, they always fall. Think of it - always."

Patience

Even though networking generally begins with a quick introduction, the actual relationship can take longer to cultivate. Sometimes it may take a year or two to gain from networking, but with diligence the reward will eventually come.

Honour Time

Recognize and value the importance of time. Manage your time well. When approaching a potential contact, be friendly, respectful and brief. When making a phone call, make a few notes on important points, so that you will not forget what to say, and it will help save time. E-mail is usually preferred over phone calls.

Reciprocate

Networking isn't about pushing oneself on to others. It is about developing mutually rewarding relationships. Every time you ask for something or meet with a potential contact, you should think about how you can help in return. If nothing else, make sure to ask how you can help the other person. In the words of Roman Emperor Markus Aurelius, "Don't go on discussing what a good person should be, "just be one."

Knowledge

The purpose of business networking is to share information, increase your visibility in your field and establish personal connections that will help you move forward in your career. Be well read and well informed about current issues, businesses, and knowledge based topics, so that you always have something interesting to share.

Approachability

Develop a likeable, genuine and considerate personality. It is easier for people to relate to a positive and pleasant person.

Follow Up

After a successful first network meeting, it's your responsibility to maintain the contact. Send a "thank you" note, within 48 hours of the meeting. *(Handwritten thank-you notes are more appreciated than emails.)*

Thereafter, find reasonable and genuine reasons to reach out. Some prefer email or a phone call, while others prefer keeping in contact through social networking service's like LinkedIn.

To maintain the contact, send a link to an interesting news story related to the individual's industry. Or, if you've identified a common interest such as a love for art or music, let them know about an opening or an upcoming event. After the gap of one month, take the initiative to invite your contact for another meeting, according to their time and convenience.

Caution

Even though, networking is the most effective way of seeking employment, it is important, to remain objective, and not depend entirely on network groups to find employment. Keep away from networking with the wrong people.

The Networking Chain

The Networking Sheet

Name_____

Address_____

Email_____

Contact No. _____

Name of organization_____

Designation_____

Details of organization_____

Details of first meeting/Reference

First meeting_____

Reference_____

Optional Information

Birthday_____

Anniversary_____

Business Card Specifications

A business card is relatively simple to print. There are some specific formats, and guidelines to be followed.

- Make sure your business card is not torn and the details are current and updated.
- A standard printed business card size is **3.5 x 2 inches.**
- Use good-quality paper and printing.

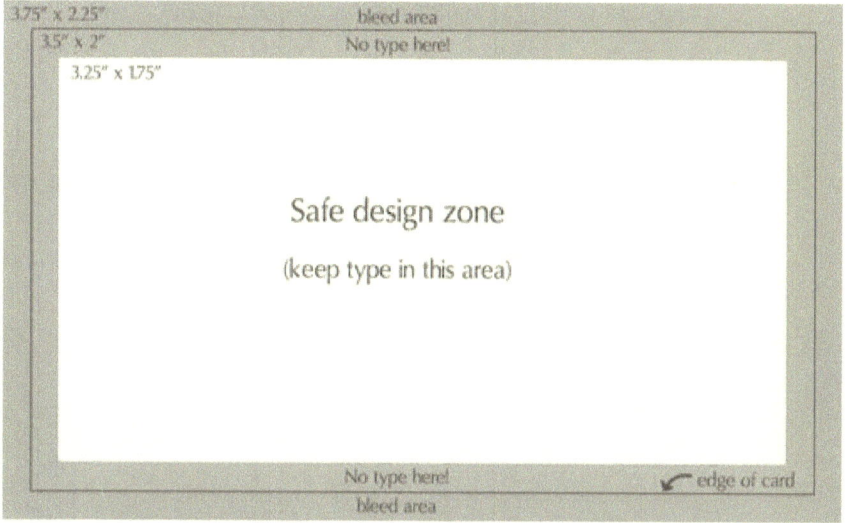

- Develop and maintain powerful relationships.
- Seek mutually rewarding associations.
- Maintain a cordial association with co-workers and clients.
- Remain involved with both formal and informal networking groups.
- Never hesitate to rebuild rapport with personal friends and professional associates.

 ## Summary

1. Make a list of all professional and personal contacts.
2. Join networking groups.
3. Once a month, attempt to volunteer in a social or community events.
4. Develop five contacts, as often as possible.
5. Make it a practice to remain in contact with your networking group through email or phone.
6. Remember to greet and wish all your contacts on special occasions, birthdays and anniversaries.

Chapter 17

Develop A Risk Management Plan

....

"Risk is like fire; if controlled it will help you; if uncontrolled it will rise up and destroy you."

– THEODORE ROOSEVELT

Safety Measures

This chapter is focused on making employees aware of the everyday risks they are exposed to in the workplace. Employees need to be made aware of the fact that all employers are legally responsible for implementing occupational health and safety rules, and take appropriate measures to protect the health and safety of all their workers.

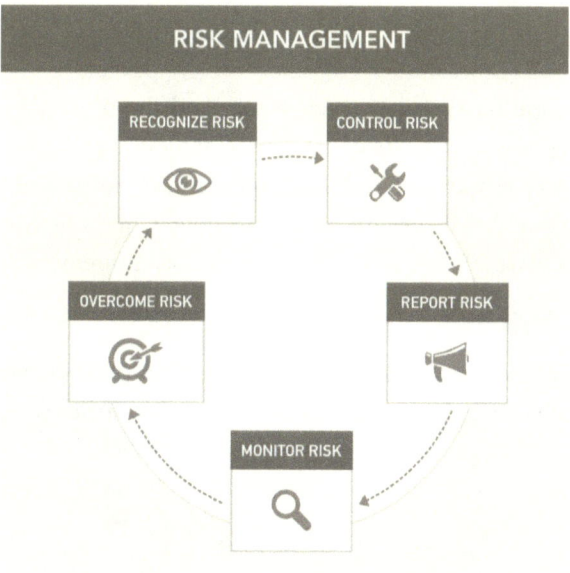

Definition of Key Terms

Hazard

A situation or machinery, material, and behavior that, has the potential to cause harm to a person. These could include overly noisy machinery, a moving forklift, toxic chemicals, electricity, working at heights, a repetitive job, bullying, and violence in the workplace.

Risk

Risk is the harm (death, injury or illness) that can take place when an employee is exposed to a particular hazard or a harmful work environment. According to American business magnate Warren Buffet, "Risk comes from not knowing what you're doing." As a result of modern industrial pollution, employees are forever exposed to heavy metals, which can cause serious health problems.

Heavy Metal Toxicity

Mercury Toxicity

Mercury is the one of the most toxic metals. It affects both the brain and the body. Symptoms of mercury toxicity include fatigue, irritability, muscular weakness and decreased immunity.

Lead Toxicity

Lead is one of the most widely used metals, and the most toxic of all metals. Too much exposure leads to the metal getting absorbed in the body. It can cause major damage to the kidney, liver, heart, and the nervous system. Water supplied through lead pipes can also cause, lead poisoning. Common symptoms of lead poisoning include irritability, fatigue, mental confusion, tremors and seizures.

Aluminum Toxicity

Aluminum in large amounts can harm the brain and the kidneys. Symptoms of aluminum toxicity include extreme nervousness, headaches, memory loss, and muscle weakness.

Metal Toxicity Test

A simple hair analysis test, done by a doctor, accurately measures the presence of toxic chemicals in your body. A small sample of the hair is sent to a medical lab. A mineral concentration in the hair is a reliable indicator of minerals present in the body. If your health, diet or environment has created a mineral imbalance or an excess of toxic minerals, this will be evident in your hair shaft.

Risk Assessment

- At the start of a new business or while purchasing a business.
- Change in the work practices, procedures or the work environment.
- Conduct due diligence during the purchase of new or used equipment, and while making use of new substances.

Risk Control

- Identify risks.
- Adopt measures to minimize workplace hazards.
- Learn to recognize the hazards and risks associated with a particular business.
- Assess the extent of the risk, and the available ways of eliminating or minimizing the risk.
- Implement the most effective control measures.
- Respond immediately to workplace incidents (even if they have caused no harm or injury).
- Do not ignore concerns raised by workers about health and safety issues in the workplace.

Role of Management

- Effective risk management starts with a commitment to health and safety from those who operate and manage the business or undertaking.
- Provide training to employees, to operate the machine and equipment safely, limit contact with hazardous tasks, and use signs to warn people of exposure to risks.
- Use measures, to provide the highest level of protection to employees, and each person, exposed to the immediate environment.
- Adopt suitable safety measures in line with the exposure to the risk and hazard.
- Undertake periodical checks of risk control measures.
- Invest time and money into high-quality health and safety equipment.
- Ensure health and safety responsibilities are clearly understood by each member of the management team.

■ The Empowered Employee

Managers and supervisors should be given the training and resources to implement and maintain control measures for a safe workplace.

- Organize regular health and safety training workshops for the employees.
- Recognizing and reporting risks must be made compulsory for all employees.
- Employees should demand and ensure the need for a risk-free environment.
- Implement a reward system to create a safe and risk-free workplace.

Summary

1. Develop awareness about the activities and situations which can cause maximum risk in the workplace.
2. Learn to respond appropriately to the risk.
3. Adopt different methods and forms of putting up caution and warning signs.
4. Train to handle risks that are specific and applicable to your organization.
5. Read the Occupational Health and Safety Act of various organizations.

Chapter 18

Dealing with Stress

"It is not stress that kills us, it is our reaction to it."

– HANS SELYE

What is stress?

Stress is the body's reaction to intense physical and emotional trauma. How you respond to the circumstances is what matters. An effective way to manage stress is by consulting a professional. Seeking help will reduce suffering, and overpower depression and fatigue.

Limited stress is beneficial; it helps in the release of powerful hormone that boosts short-term efficiency during emergency situations. Long-term exposure to stress causes the automatic release of the hormone cortisol in the brain. This condition can lead to a number of disorders including strokes and, blood pressure, and obstruct learning.

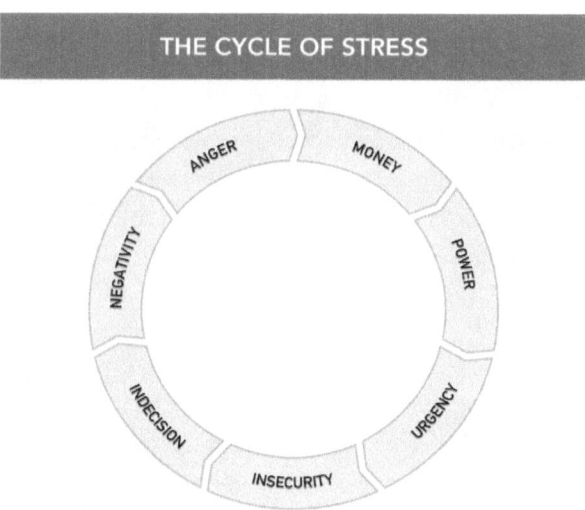

Anger

The primary cause of stress is anger. Letting go of self-control will leave you in a state of extreme vulnerability, giving rise to fear and negative emotions. You must train your mind to overcome, the emotion of fear, before it controls you. It is impossible to control the negative actions of others. However, we can control our responses with self-discipline, composure and common sense.

Money

The most important factor, contributing to stress is money. It is essential, not to become a slave to excessive material desires. The question is, how to achieve this in a highly competitive, and materially driven world. A survey commissioned in America found that seventy-three percent of the population single out money as the most significant factor that contributes to stress. To be resilient, is an effective way of handling adversity and trauma that includes day-to-day family, health, workplace or financial problems. Anyone can learn how to cope with stress with practice, determination and hard work.

Power

Power is a form of authority everyone desires to have. Power is not necessarily always negative. It depends, on the individual who uses it. There are a number of ways in which power, can manifest itself. - And for this reason, it's important to realize, that power exists in all of us.

The two biggest blunders of using indiscriminate power are the following:

➢ Attempting to forcefully, exert power over others.
➢ Using the wrong kind of power to achieve results.

To help you identify your 'power zone', (refer to chapter 9), take a moment and think about how you can exert influence over others. Use the above description as a self-assessment tool to influence your thoughts and actions. Rate yourself on a scale of 1-5 in the two different kinds of power. Getting over the fear of the loss of power will reduce stress.

Urgency

A sense of urgency places, unrealistic demands upon us, resulting in stress, and severe anxiety. Individuals, who remain in a state of constant urgency create self-imposed stressors. Medical and occupational researchers have found a strong correlation between urgency, and lack of job performance.

Insecurity

Never become a victim of insecurity, as a result of a peer's success or any other. Insecurity in the workplace can destroy a successful career. A feeling of insecurity will begin to dominate your personality, leading to inefficiency. Rise above the feeling of insecurity with determination and self-confidence. You will be surprised at how quickly you can change negative thoughts into a positive feeling.

- Conduct a self-assessment, to reflect on your insecurities and strengths.
- Set goals, to help build self-confidence. Focus on setting both achievable and challenging goals.
- Take additional steps to overcome your insecurities. Participate in training or team-building programs.
- Always think positively, avoid self-criticism, and banish negative thoughts and fears.

Indecision

Indecision causes more stress and grief. Ms. Gretchen Rubin, one of the most influential writers on habits and happiness, and author of *The Happiness Project* and *Happier at Home* shares two thought-proving decision-making styles.

Satisfiers are those who take action once they narrow down their choices. This does not mean they lower their standards. They assess their options and make good decisions.

Maximizers are unreasonable perfectionists. Persons who fall in this category are prone to changing their mind even after having made a decision because they end up feeling unhappy about it. They tend to remain more depressed. Maximizers would be happier if they brought a little more perspective and accept both major and minor decisions with a sense of satisfaction.

In her most recent book, *Better Than Before*, she acquaints the readers on how to develop habits that will transform their lives, even if they've failed before.

Most people fall in the middle category. A good option, rather than waiting is to select a preference, analyze to a reasonable level and then trust your intuition. The best decisions are made when logical reasoning and gut feeling are balanced out.

Negativity

Negativity or negative stress occurs, when the body is not able to return to a relaxed state, even in the absence of the stressor. It has been scientifically proven;

people who focus on the negative are more prone to depression, and other mental health disorders.

Signs and Symptoms of Stress

A stress-related panic attack can also be a warning sign of a heart attack. Any of the following physical symptoms should be immediately reported to a doctor.

Emotional	Physical	Cognitive
Frustration	Rapid Heartbeat	Hampers Learning
Indecision	Chest Pain	Loss of Memory
Isolation	Heavy Breathing	Negative Self-Talk
Depression	Influenza	Confusion
Mood Disorders	Bacterial Infection	Nervousness
Unhappy Relationships	Lack of Immunity	Tense Muscles

Mind, Body and Soul Connection

Career balance and success, depends on maintaining equilibrium between the mind, body and soul. A person who can keep a balance between the mind, body and soul is a strong and happy person. Whether you are seeking peace of mind, or your life's purpose, countless cells in your body are carrying out millions of infinitely complex operations to keep you alive.

Even though we constantly try to banish negative thoughts, the human brain simply doesn't have a mechanism for doing it without a positive disposition. Psychologists call this the ironic thought process, whereby deliberate attempts to suppress certain thoughts, return merely because we try not to think about them.

Challenge your mind to expand, grow, learn and experience. One who can keep a balanced mind at all times remains calm, grounded, clear-headed and motivated. To sum it up in one sentence, **"Suffering is not caused by pain but by resisting pain"**~Unknown

Effective Ways to Eliminate Stress

The author suggests a unique approach to overcome stress other than a change in lifestyle, and conventional treatment methods. To start with, long-term stress can be handled with a change in thinking. Confront complex situations with determination and optimism. Build inner strength to overcome challenges and countless setbacks.

Spin Failure into Success

In 1914, Thomas Alva Edison's, laboratory burned down. His laboratory was priceless; nearly all of his life's work was completely destroyed. When other people offered their condolences, he responded by saying, "All our mistakes are burned up, now we can start new." Three weeks later, he invented the phonograph.

Turn Collapse into Reassurance

Nothing is impossible. No matter what the issue, the way you handle it is the key to resolving a situation. Train your mind to think in a positive way and not become a helpless victim of your circumstances. The power is in your willingness to make the change and overcome resistance. Your intelligence will make you persist and create a future of hope and fulfilment. According to a study most patients need reassuring words to make a U-turn from sickness to healing.

Transfer Poverty to Wealth

The greatest example is that of Oprah Winfrey. She overcame extreme childhood poverty to establish herself as a leading celebrity in the entertainment industry. Recalling her childhood experience, she once told her viewers, "When I look into the future, it's so bright, it burns my eyes."

Change Vulnerability to Strength

Achieving excellence is not a skill, but an attitude on how to overcome failure, and turn it to our advantage. Rightly described, in the words of Eleanor Roosevelt, "We gain strength, courage, and confidence by each experience in which we really stop to look fear in the face, and we must do what we think we cannot."

Switch Insecurity to Confidence

The feeling of insecurity is the core of the misery of a lot of problems and suffering. We can have power over our insecurities by creating harmony and balance between our inner thoughts and beliefs. Our resistance to change is a way of losing peace and happiness. Switching insecurity to confidence is a new way of dealing with stress. It is vital to understand that, with confidence one can awaken new ways of overcoming insecurity deeply buried within us. Even though our resistance comes up strong, confidence overpowers the mind to overcome anxiety in any situation or condition.

Exchange Procrastination for Motivation

Procrastinating over circumstances makes us do things that make us unaware of the consequences. Procrastination impacts your entire life. It breaks the cycle, sets back time and makes everything look like failure. It over-generalizes both the advantages and disadvantages of a situation.

The fear of taking a decision lets go of vital opportunities. The best approach is to go out there and make the mistakes, if you land in a bad situation do not regret it. Accept the fact that every individual has the ability to deal with failure. Remain motivated and build the courage to attempt it again until you reach the stage of perfection. Each mistake makes you learn something new, leading to long-term benefits. This approach makes life easier in the long term.

- Think clearly and stay focused under pressure.
- Overcome self-hatred and a victim mentality.
- Focus on the task at hand.
- Rise above the danger of stagnation.
- Moderate anxiety mobilizes action and energizes the body.
- Always remain in touch with your subconscious mind. This conveys powerful and crucial messages.
- Deal with difficult situations in a straightforward manner.

Summary

1. Exercise regularly, practise yoga and meditation.
2. Read motivational books.
3. Learn to relax with the help of music, sports or any other form of entertainment.
4. Surround yourself with happy and positive people.
5. Get enough sleep and eat a well-balanced diet.

Chapter 19

Team Building in the Workplace

"Talent wins games, but teamwork and intelligence wins championships."
– MICHAEL JORDAN

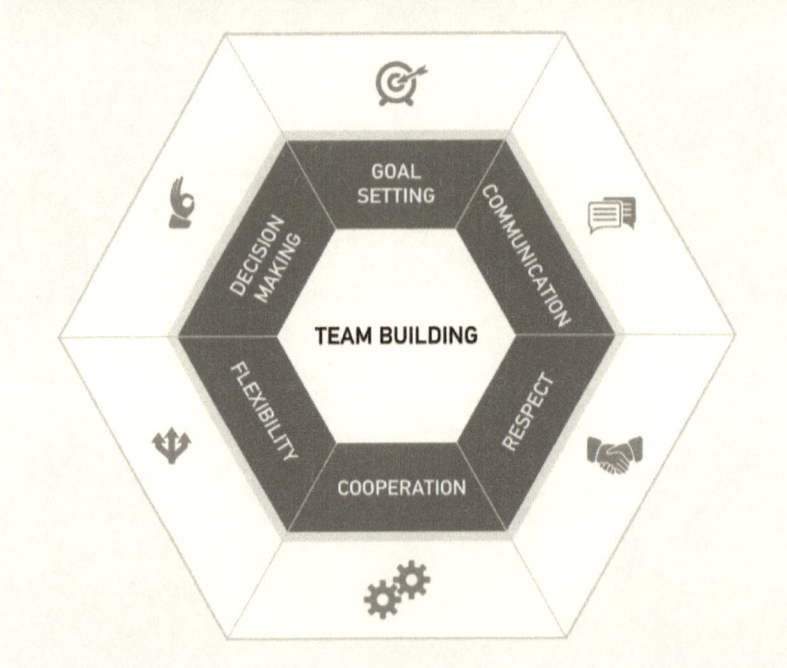

Goal Setting

Team building takes place when a group of employees set a specific goal. As the team begins to take shape, it becomes the responsibility of every team member to achieve the goal. The Chief Executive Officer of a large telecom company defines their team-building initiative as "Our approach to team-building is to connect our team with a passionate sense of shared **"purpose"**- we make this possible through focused discussion, communication and creative ideas."

Communication

Communication skills such as listening, patience and empathy are of extreme importance. Supportive team members create an environment to communicate effectively with each other. Pride, prejudice, and insecurity cause numerous hurdles. Problem solving and creating thinking is possible only through positive interaction.

Respect

A team is a collaboration between individuals based on interdependence. The team lead operates on the mutual exchange of thoughts and ideas. Forming amicable relationships helps cultivate the right behavior and attitude within the team. According to a senior executive of a leading oil company, respect and trust are two vital aspects for a leader to build a successful team. He says, "Team building has many key elements; the two most important being trust and respect."

Cooperation

Everyone knows the power of thinking "we" instead of "me". A shared vision brings collective commitment and success. It enhances understanding, helps achieve common interests, and furthers creativity, intelligence and persuasive skills into one integrated whole. Winning is fun, but winning together is more fun. Synergy in a diverse workforce can create infinite possibilities by combining common forces, or leveraging opposing ones.

Flexibility

The ability to adapt to change helps a team grow both individually and as a group. The lack of flexibility leads to a loss of resources and output. Margaret Mead, author and speaker, states, *"Never doubt that a small group of thoughtful, committed people can change the world. Indeed, it is the only thing that ever has."*

Decision Making

Teams are particularly good in problem solving where they make "good" decisions. A leader must recognize the problem that exists and identify the real issue. Once the problem is defined, team members need to brainstorm and explore various solutions to the problem, objectively weighing and anticipating the outcome. All members must participate and express their opinions. Members must share the responsibility as a team and implement the collective decision.

Rules for Effective Team Management

Leadership

Similar to a football game, it is a fine bonding experience. Encouraging teamwork is an essential business skill. A good leader inspires and creates an environment of respect within the team.

Organization

A competent leader focuses on problem solving and creative thinking, sets clear priorities and carefully considers the risks. They take the initiative to build an interdependent workforce based on common behaviors, outlook and attitude.

Wisdom

A leader is instrumental in the overall development of a team by creating an environment of action and practical wisdom. They often focus on building an organization to achieve excellence and greater efficiency.

Mediation

An effective way to resolve conflict is through mediation. The leader needs to sit with each member of the team in private to address their concerns and identify areas of common interest. In such matters, it is important for the leader to remain unbiased and impartial.

Performance

A team often experiences the feeling of perceived failure. This happens more frequently when members begin to doubt their ability to execute a particular task. The switch from contemplation to action, often leads to "performance anxiety". To be successful a leader needs to identify a "Star Performer". This role should be assigned according to experience and past performance. A realistic approach helps in achieving practical results and high performance.

TIPS

- Identify the strengths and transferable skills of each team member.
- Set specific targets to accomplish goals.
- Focus to gain a competitive advantage.
- A manager should encourage feedback from each team member.

Summary

1. Find innovative ways to enhance teamwork and build team spirit.
2. Learn teamwork and problem-solving skills.
3. Strengthen your ability to build a cohesive and functional team.
4. Train to manage the different stages of team building.
5. Practice and participate in fun and challenging team exercises.

Chapter 20

Strategies to Resolve Conflict

"An eye for an eye will only make the whole world blind."

– MAHATMA GANDHI

The most difficult issue prevailing in the workplace is about resolving conflicts. A sense of superiority, prejudice, pride and vanity gives rise to disagreements. During a conflict the first reaction is always of anger. The key to resolving a conflict is to find the real reason behind the disagreement. Never put people on the defensive, and avoid criticism and personal remarks. Let the person justify themselves. This can include a boss, peer, client, subordinate or a customer.

A forgetful gesture such as looking through a person or not reacting to what one says can lead to unpleasant encounters in real-life situations. Conflicts often happen where people have the highest level of ambition and the craze of limitless material things. Always remain watchful of hostile behavior from seniors and peers.

Effective Conflict-Solving Techniques

Acceptance

A realistic approach is to accept and identify the reason behind the conflict. There may be many hidden causes which may give rise to a chain of unpleasant events. Step out of the situation and recall a state when you may have reacted in a similar manner. The fact is in some instances you may have to swallow your pride, accept the real situation and acknowledge your weakness. Minimize emotional responses. Increase your ability to handle difficult situations. Prepare to take appropriate action and be willing to do it alone. For this you will be admired and respected.

Response

Thinking about what needs to be done, increases your ability to cope with difficult situations. Know for sure what the facts are, and how they fit together. Plan for unplanned and unconscious reactions, mobilized by anxiety and anger. Emotions are usually involved and need a fair amount of time to subside.

Aggression needs time to settle. When you find the behavior of a person overly difficult to handle, understand why people behave in the manner they do. Delay your response if you have nothing positive to say. Be watchful of those who are incompetent, over sensitive and weak. If they turn aggressive by yelling or crying awkwardly, give them time to overcome their hostile behavior.

Influence

Persuasion requires the highest level of competency. It needs productive and powerful thinking strategies, through logic and reasonable judgment. You need to control the situation in a way for them to recognize that you will not respond according to their hostile and unreasonable behavior. After knowing the facts, suggest a reasonable solution to the crisis. This approach is likely to pay off in the long run.

Communication

Honest and clear communication works like magic. In an environment of open communication, people are less frightened of spilling out the real facts. A positive and confident approach, with a clear purpose, helps resolve the problem to everyone's best interest.

Avoid criticism and personal attacks as most people you meet will have a sense of insecurity and some level of anxiety present in them. Give people the right to speak and express their point of view. According to research conducted, it is better to be seated while resolving a conflict, as while sitting most people are less likely to be aggressive.

Patience

Exercising patience can play a key role in resolving a conflict. Do not feel disappointed if the conflict does not resolve in the first attempt. Dealing with people in a multicultural workplace requires tremendous patience. Listening attentively and being patient with persons who throw tantrums gives them an opportunity to overcome their emotional outburst and become normal.

■ The Empowered Employee

Try to build a consensus, with a group of people, willing to resolve the conflict amicably. Be watchful of whom you trust to be your aides in resolving a conflict. Some people may show they are in agreement with your plan, but let you down eventually. However, none of this suggests that you should expose yourself to continuing hostile and unreasonable behavior.

Temporary Withdrawal

Withdrawing completely from a situation may be interpreted as not having a solution to the problem. A positive response in a negative situation brings about better results. However, if the situation is more severe, withdrawing temporarily may be a better option, gather the facts, and let the aggression subside. Focus on the real issue and resolve it with a long-term solution to the problem.

Solution

Put forward a reasonable solution, thereafter wait for the reaction. Avoid proposing a solution in haste. Generate multiple alternatives. Human behavior is too broad; no single and ordinary approach works. Contrary to popular belief, being overly anxious to resolve a conflict can lead to further escalation. Avoid giving anyone preferential treatment, including yourself. Remain true to your values and intentions. Even then there are may be less chances of total agreement between individuals involved in the conflict. A compromise where appropriate suggestions are put into action is the best solution.

TIPS

- Try to remain free of aggressive behavior.
- Maintain cordial and positive relationships at work.
- Control the urge to react in an aggressive manner.
- Keep yourself motivated to solve conflicts in every situation.

# *Summary*

1. Train to resolve conflicts.
2. Become skilled at dealing with complex situations in the workplace.
3. Attempt to control the impact of stress and fear in your life.
4. Learn to identify and handle the potentially devastating impact of unresolved conflicts.
5. Develop the ability to handle conflicts caused by emotional outbursts.

REFERENCES

Daniel Goleman, *Author - Emotional Intelligence: "Why It Can Matter More Than IQ"*

I am grateful to Daniel Golemen, for the permission to reference his breakthrough concept of Emotional Intelligence in this book.

Gretchen Rubin, *Author - The Happiness Project/Better than Before*

Thank you for granting me permission, to include your thought-provoking ideas on habits, happiness and human nature.

Dr. Martin E.P. Seligman, – A special word of gratitude to Dr. Martin E.P. Seligman, for the outstanding support with the **Seligman Attributional Style Questionnaire (SASQ),** the unique testing method for Emotional Intelligence.

David Calver, - I wish to express, a sincere thank you to David Calver, editor and proof reader for the diligence, and extra effort to make my book the best it can be.

www.ingramcontent.com/pod-product-compliance
Lightning Source LLC
Chambersburg PA
CBHW020426220526
45464CB00002B/585